D1557502

Plato through Homer

PLATO
THROUGH
HOMER

POETRY AND PHILOSOPHY
IN THE
COSMOLOGICAL DIALOGUES

Zdravko Planinc

UNIVERSITY OF MISSOURI PRESS
COLUMBIA AND LONDON

Copyright © 2003 by
The Curators of the University of Missouri
University of Missouri Press, Columbia, Missouri 65201
Printed and bound in the United States of America
All rights reserved
5 4 3 2 1   07 06 05 04 03

Library of Congress Cataloging-in-Publication Data

Planinc, Zdravko, 1953-
Plato through Homer : poetry and philosophy in the cosmological dialogues
/ Zdravko Planinc.
   p.   cm.
Includes bibliographical references and index.
ISBN 0-8262-1479-7 (alk. paper)
1. Plato. Dialogues.   2. Homer. Odyssey.   1. Title.
B395 .P514 2003
184–dc21
   2003009987

⊚™   This paper meets the requirements of the
American National Standard for Permanence of Paper
for Printed Library Materials, Z39.48, 1984.

Text Designer: Stephanie Foley
Jacket Designer: Susan Ferber
Typesetter: BOOKCOMP
Printer and Binder: Thomson-Shore, Inc.
Typefaces: Palatino and Weissach

For Oona

You are quite right: [Stefan] George understood more of
Plato than did Wilamowitz, Jaeger, and the whole gang.

—Leo Strauss to Eric Voegelin, letter of June 4, 1951

DEXIMENES: Plato knows he will never be a great poet.
PLATO: I'm going to destroy all my poems—tonight—I'll
tear them up!
SOCRATES: Now, now, my children, be at peace, and
don't tear things up, especially not poems.

—Iris Murdoch, *Art and Eros*

Socrates and Plato—
They praised it to the skies

—Van Morrison, "I Forgot That Love Existed,"
Poetic Champions Compose

Contents

Acknowledgments

There is an undeniable tactile pleasure in handling the volumes of the *Loeb Classical Library* (Harvard University Press). I have used them for the Greek texts throughout, except on the few occasions when the *Perseus Digital Library* (Classics Department, Tufts University) was more convenient. In translating and paraphrasing Plato and Homer, I have also consulted Richmond Lattimore's *Odyssey* (Harper and Row), Allan Bloom's *Republic* (Basic Books), Seth Benardete's *Symposium* (University of Chicago Press), James Nichols's *Phaedrus* (Cornell University Press), and Francis Cornford's *Plato's Cosmology* (Bobbs-Merrill).

Earlier versions of parts of this study were presented to the Philosophy and Political Science Departments at McMaster University, to the Political Science Department at the Univer-

sity of Calgary, and to meetings of the Society for Greek Political Thought, the Canadian Political Science Association, and
the American Political Science Association. My thanks to all
involved. Thanks are also due to Beverly Jarrett, the director
of the University of Missouri Press, who has been unwavering
in her support of my project, and to Jane Lago and Annette
Wenda, my patient and thoroughgoing editors.

The best discussions of Plato and Homer take place in settings and circumstances comparable to those described in the
dialogues and in the more hospitable and intimate episodes of
the *Odyssey*—gatherings in which everyone who participates
has something at stake, no matter whether the encounter is
unexpected and spontaneous, or part of an everyday routine,
or a long-anticipated appointment: speaking with a teacher,
or with students; a conversation with friends; affable quarrels
with poets and businessmen; less frequently, chats with fellow
academics that circumvent the safeguards of collegiality; and
no encounter more welcome and fulfilling than talking with
the ones you love. In ways that I cannot begin to acknowledge
adequately, many such discussions have shaped my readings
of the texts and contributed to what I have at stake in this work.

And so many other things too, each clamoring to be recognized. The years of a misspent youth, playing in a rock group
that the drummer, for reasons unknown, insisted be named Atlantis. Slipping into a nightclub as a minor to listen to Miles
Davis and the *Bitches Brew* band; or listening to Charles Mingus
toward the end of his life in a nearly empty basement bar; or to
Bill Evans whenever he brought a trio to town. Reading through
chess games by Aron Nimzowitsch and Alexander Alekhine,
and risking what I'd learned in Wednesday-night tournaments.
Books: books discovered accidentally; Alice Kane's libraries
and stories; surprising books received as presents from passing
acquaintances and distant relatives. Learning to read Shakespeare with a Welshman, thank God. Watching François Truf-
faut's *400 Blows* for the first time, or Martin Scorsese's *Mean
Streets*, or Bernardo Bertolucci's *Conformist*. Seeing the North-
ern Lights; the Rockies and the Prairies; moonrise at a borrowed
cottage in the Kawarthas; a stone, a leaf, a door.

Plato through Homer

Journeys

Plato and Homer

From its first word—*katebēn,* "I went down"—Plato's *Republic* remains unfamiliar to us. When we do not consider the dialogue closely, it seems quite familiar. We are satisfied that we know the broad features of its argument; we might also know something of the history of its interpretation, perhaps sharing one of the many colorful opinions that have been expressed about Plato's political theory; and the rest, we think, is surely either philological detail or antique embellishment. However, the striking manner in which Socrates' first remark is presented should unsettle our confidence. It cannot be a minor detail that Plato has Socrates recollect the entirety of the previous night's discussions and narrate it, in his own voice, to an unidentified auditor. And it cannot be an insignificant literary ornament

that Plato has Socrates begin by alluding to the scene in the
Odyssey in which Odysseus, finally reunited with Penelope,
tells her of his long travels and the hardships yet to come, as
he heard of them from Teiresias,

> on that day
> when I went down *(katebēn)* inside the house of
>   Hades, seeking
> to learn about homecoming, for myself and my
>   companions.
>
> (*Odyssey* 23.251–53)

The mix of familiarity and discomfort raised in us when we
pause over any of Plato's dialogues has its roots in tradition. At
one time, knowing of the existence of the *Republic* was a rare
thing. For most of a thousand years, all of Plato in the West was
a partial Latin translation of the *Timaeus*, serving as a proof text
for theologians' claims that even the best of the ancient Greeks
were merely natural philosophers who knew nothing of divine
revelation and its consequences. During the Renaissance, the
Greek texts of all the dialogues were recovered, and Marsilio
Ficino took up the project of translating them into Latin that
had been abandoned with the death of Boethius. The Florentine
Academy sought to recapture the spirit of Plato's Academy,
but its attempts to reconcile Plato and Christianity succeeded
only in replacing a tradition of indifference and neglect with
enthusiastic accommodation. In recent times, all of the dialogues have become available in every vernacular. Yet something about them continues to escape us. Taken individually,
each dialogue seems an oddity, and we have no convincing
synoptic understanding of them all. Why would the author of
the *Republic* also write the *Laws*? Why write the *Timaeus* as well
as the *Phaedrus*? How can the *Symposium* be reconciled with any
other dialogue? And why is the *Euthydemus* not considered as
brilliant as the *Gorgias* or the *Protagoras*? Let scholars distract
themselves with such peripheral matters; our understanding
of Plato is sufficient for our purposes, we assume. And so, the
tradition of accommodation and neglect continues.

The civilization of ancient Greece does not touch us directly. It is a ruins, the beautiful fragments of which occasionally move us to pick them up and consider them with curiosity, but never out of the light of the present things that concern us more. Its buildings and its books have shared a similar fate. The Parthenon, for instance, was remodeled as both a church and a mosque in the Middle Ages; it then became a powder magazine in early modern times, with disastrous results; more recently, it served as the source of the "Elgin Marbles," artifacts of a moribund museum culture, if not of a broader justification for empire; and now, it is a posthistorical tourist site, suitable for New Age concerts. The ancient city of Troy did not fare any the better for having avoided such treatment. It lay forgotten for centuries until Heinrich Schliemann excavated it, acting on the academically scandalous notion that Homer's *Iliad* could be read seriously. The few scholars from whom Schliemann took the idea—Charles Maclaren, George Grote, and others—have now become legions of archaeologists who no longer read the *Iliad* solely as poetry, even if they lack something of the audacity that sought out Homer's Troy in the first place.

We are separated from ancient Greece by Rome, the new Troy, in which the *Iliad* and *Odyssey* were no more than quaint source texts for Virgil's *Aeneid,* and Plato, a little-known precursor of Cicero. We are separated from it by Christian Rome, in which the Bible and Augustine's *City of God* superseded all pagan poetry and philosophy. The Renaissance also distances us: for all its homage to the Greeks, it sought the rebirth of Rome, not Athens. And after the debacle of the modern world's mad attempts to found New Romes and New Jerusalems, we are so far removed from ancient Greece that even the cultural glories of the Renaissance seem unapproachable to us. Raphael's painting for the Vatican's papal apartments, for example, *The School of Athens,* portrays an assembly of ancient philosophers, many of whose figures cannot be identified with any certainty, in an arrangement the iconography of which remains a matter of speculation, though we know it to have been influenced by the Florentine Academy. Nearby, the Vatican's Sistine Chapel has recently been cleaned and restored, removing the penumbra of dirt, soot, and animal glue that had for centuries obscured the brilliant colors of Michelangelo's frescoes more effectively than subsequent touch-ups had covered over his nudes. But it was not done without protest from traditionalists. There will always be those who prefer not to consider original things without the mediation of a tradition, and those who prefer the things that separate us from beauty to looking at the beautiful itself.

When we wish to honor the man, we often say that the history of philosophy is nothing but a series of footnotes to Plato. Far from it: Plato is seldom more than a footnote in the works of others. In his *Essays* (2.12), Michel de Montaigne observed that "all sorts of learned authors" use references to authoritative texts—the Bible, Homer's epics, Plato's dialogues—as little more than rhetorical ballast for their own views: "See how Plato is tossed and turned about. All are honored to have his support, so they couch him on their own side. They trot him out and slip him into any new opinion which fashion will accept. When matters take a different turn, then they make him disagree with himself. . . . The more powerful and vigorous the mind of his interpreters, the more vigorously and powerfully they do it."[1] Interpretations of Plato's dialogues need not be arbitrary, but all too often they are. "Plato" is a name to be conjured with, the magical power of which increases with the irrelevance of his works to the things that most deeply affect us.

In Western civilization there are at least three collections of writings, each of which may be said to express the full range of human experience and the greatest possible openness to the several horizons that define the human condition: Plato's dialogues, the Bible, and Shakespeare's plays. Although everyone has likely suffered encounters with forced readings of the other two, I think it would be fair to say that Plato's dialogues are the most abused. The Bible and Shakespeare's plays are texts that are interpreted, and indeed lived, within popular institutions—temples and theaters—that continue to have a place, however

1. Michel de Montaigne, *The Complete Essays*, trans. M. A. Screech (London: Penguin, 1991), 662.

tenuous, in modern society. The dialogues have no comparable institutional embodiment: certainly not the modern university, organized as it is around technologically driven research
in the sciences. In the easy confidence that our civilization has
subsumed the best of the Greeks and surpassed the worst, we
allow ourselves the conceit of naming the modern university
after Plato's Academy, but there is nothing Platonic about it.

In our Academy, Plato's dialogues remain an undiscovered
country more often fantastically described than explored,
though the borders prevent no one from crossing. Their richness is not hidden from view; it lies in plain sight, but it remains
unseen. Perhaps this is only to be expected. The vast numbers
of biblical scholars and Shakespearian scholars regularly oc-
cupied in the intricacies of textual interpretation do not often
claim to have penetrated the heart of their text's mystery. If a
hermeneutic "fusion of horizons" with a profound text—one
that calls every aspect of the reader's own life experience into
question—is inherently difficult to attain, and if the entire en-
deavor for an intellectual is beset with distracting problems
caused by the necessity of working within the parameters of
established scholarship, it is quite understandable that Plato's
dialogues would have relatively few serious academic readers.

And yet, what prodigious industry is applied to tossing Plato
about in the university. The dialogues are studied as peculiar
philological artifacts, fragmented into passages—sometimes
topical, sometimes not—and then endlessly puzzled back together again. The criteria for reconstructing them come and go:
historical references, grammatical patterns, speculation about
what it must have been like for Plato to get old—it seems everything has been tried. Some methods are deliberately extrinsic to
the dialogues: they are reread through Kant's eyes, or through
Augustine's eyes, or through the lenses of any number of other
well-known interpretive schemes or up-to-the-moment ideo-
logical orientations in a wearying search for traces of novelty.
The most venerable research program is the hunt for a definition of Plato's "Platonism." Libraries have gathered extensive
collections of such studies, each of which provides its author's
favorite recipe for mixing ingredients that are found readily

enough in the dialogues: Eleatic theorizing, Pythagorean philosophy, and straight sophistry, with perhaps a dash of Socrates' refutative method, the *elenchos*, added to taste.

There is an immediate charm to reading Plato. It might wane
a bit in the more technical passages. However, it is almost impossible to recall ever having been enchanted by Plato when
reading most studies of him. To recapture the original experience, it is best simply to begin again. There is no need to
backtrack through the missteps of even the best-known scholarly works. Many of their divergences do not begin at the main
path, and the intricate maze they have built up over the centuries is too troublesome to fight through. Plato should be read
for enjoyment, as Shakespeare is. The dialogues are works of
literature, crafted as carefully as any of Shakespeare's tragedies
or comedies. They are not failed attempts to write Plotinus's
Enneads or Wittgenstein's *Tractatus Logico-Philosophicus*. The
aesthetic pleasure of reading the dialogues is one of the best
guides to discovering their meaning. If our understanding of
the dialogues were to be compared to our estimation of the
Sistine Chapel, then a cleaning is long overdue. The beauty of
their bold colors and graceful composition should be seen and
appreciated without the penumbra of tradition and scholarship
that has obscured them all this time. And if one were to take
up the *Republic* again, reading it in this spirit, its first word—
katebēn, "I went down"—would be immediately engaging. Socrates recounts the previous night's discussions to an unidentified auditor, and to the reader, just as Odysseus recounts his
many journeys to Penelope. Odysseus does not lie to Penelope
because she recognizes him for who he is. And she recognizes
him and understands the meaning of his words because she
loves him. To anyone else, Odysseus is nothing but a Cretan
liar. So too, the meaning of Socrates' words becomes evident to
those who recognize him and love him. To anyone else, he is
little more than a disagreeable fraud.

In one of the concluding discussions of the *Republic*, Socrates mentions an "old quarrel between philosophy and poetry" (607a). Almost nothing is known about who took part in the "old quarrel" and what their arguments were. Socrates' remark is most likely a reference to disputes about the meaning of the *Iliad* and *Odyssey* between the Pythagoreans, who were the first to call themselves "philosophers," and the Homeric rhapsodes who both performed and interpreted the epics publicly. Be that as it may, the remark certainly does not allow us to claim that the *Republic* begins the "old quarrel." The dialogue does not even provide us with an unambiguous criterion by which we might differentiate philosophy from poetry. It is true that Plato has Socrates and his interlocutors spend some of the night criticizing poetry, and especially Homer, "the most poetic and first of the tragic poets" (607b). However, Socrates also admits to having "a certain friendship for Homer" since his youth (595b). Indeed, he is a "lover of poetry" who is "charmed" to contemplate things "through Homer" (607c–d). Socrates' confession is Plato's confession as well. Later thinkers have often claimed to know better what wisdom is, taking up sides in a new quarrel between philosophy and science. They would all agree that the literary character of the dialogues is the best evidence that Plato is the most poetic and the first of the tragic philosophers.

Scholars generally allow that there is a mix of poetry and philosophy in the dialogues. Their disagreements begin when they attempt to extract the latter from the former, and they often become so involved in the details of which passages or arguments count as philosophy proper that the main difficulty in interpreting Plato is entirely overlooked. The modern understanding of the nature of philosophy leads us to think there is a self-evident distinction between philosophy and poetry, but Plato's understanding of philosophy is fundamentally different. In its highest form, it is indistinguishable from the best poetry.

Consider what is said in the *Phaedrus*, the dialogue with perhaps the most obvious poetic or literary qualities in its composition. Plato has Socrates describe and compare four kinds of "divine madness" *(mania)*; and in his ranking, the madness of poets, inspired by the Muses, is second only to the madness of philosophers, inspired by Eros (244a ff). Then, when Socrates ranks nine kinds of human soul, he says the highest and best is the soul of "a philosopher, or a lover of beauty, or a music and erotic [soul]." True poets have music souls, unlike the wordsmiths whose souls rank sixth, and true philosophers have essentially similar ones, unlike the intellectuals or sophists whose souls are eighth, only slightly above tyrants (248d–e). Finally, at the conclusion of the dialogue, Socrates suggests that his arguments be used to determine if any of the men thought to be wise is worthy of the name "philosopher." He mentions Lysias and the speechwriters, Homer and the poets, Solon and the politicians, Isocrates and other promising students (278b–279b). Only Homer seems worthy of the honor: he is certainly a lover of beauty and a music and erotic man. The *Phaedrus* thus shows Plato's friendship for Homer. Philosophy and poetry, at their best, are reconciled; there is no quarrel between them.

It is not common these days to think that the highest activity of the mind and soul is erotic madness or an unmediated relation to divinity. Our understanding of the autonomy of human reason has as its concomitant a fundamental antithesis or dichotomy between what is rational and what is irrational. On this assumption, "philosophy" is sagacity, wisdom, a science— the study of the internal consistency of reasoning, modeled after logic's study of the internal consistency of speech. Anything that cannot be circumscribed by this boundary is dismissed as the supernatural, the enthusiastic, the absurd. There is no place in philosophy for poetry.

Modern understandings of the relation between reason and the irrational are always being read into the "old quarrel between philosophy and poetry." And since the premise that the rational and the irrational are antithetically opposed does not preclude there being a great many different ways of making the distinction, there are in fact a great many different reconstructions of Plato's "philosophy," all of which somehow manage to miss the point. Plato has now been modernized and postmodernized by scholars as thoroughly as he was alternately

damned and baptized by Christian theologians. It matters little whether the criterion for interpreting Plato is the distinction,
favored by most philologists, between analytic "content" and
dispensable literary "form";[2] or the argument favored by the
followers of Leo Strauss that poetry (or myth or religion) and
philosophy are antithetical accounts of "the whole," derived
from the fundamental difference in human nature between un-
reflective belief and reflective criticism;[3] or even the claim of
many postmodern theorists that the irrationality underlying
poetry is liberating and thus makes for better philosophy than
"philosophy."[4] Much of importance has been learned from the
interpretive efforts made along these lines, of course: there are
no longer any significant philological problems preventing us
from understanding the texts; we are now aware that the dialogic or conversational aspects of the texts cannot be ignored if
we are to understand them properly; and it has become obvious that the freedom with which we interpret the dialogues is
a mirror held up to our natures. And yet the dialogues largely
remain a mystery to us.

It is by reading the dialogues as works of literature that we
might best begin to understand Plato, as it were, on his own
terms. If a distinction between poetry and philosophy, or form
and content, is impossible to avoid in interpreting Plato, let it
initially be a benign one. The dialogues may be studied in two
related aspects: how they are written, and what they mean to
say. In any well-written text, the writing indicates and becomes
transparent for the saying, the meaning. In the dialogues,

2. A great number of works could be cited as examples. Let one stand
for all: Gregory Vlastos, *Platonic Studies* (Princeton: Princeton University
Press, 1981).

3. See Leo Strauss, *The City and Man* (Chicago: Rand McNally, 1964);
and Allan Bloom, "Interpretive Essay," in his edition of *The "Republic" of
Plato* (New York: Basic Books, 1968), 307–436.

4. Postmodern hermeneutical and deconstructive approaches are both
founded on the work of Martin Heidegger. Heidegger presents his analyses as scientifically rigorous, but his faux philology does not mask the "poetic" excesses of his textual interpretations too well. Consider his "Plato's
Doctrine of Truth," in *Pathways*, ed. W. McNeill (Cambridge: Cambridge
University Press, 1998), 155–82.

especially so: Plato's crafting of the written texts becomes
transparent for the words spoken by Socrates in conversation
with others, and the spoken words in turn become transparent
for an understanding of what moves the interlocutors to speak.
The poetic or literary qualities of the dialogues thus reveal the
Socratic qualities of Plato's philosophy. Eventually we come to
understand that the Music *mania* that produced their literary
form is essentially the same as the Erotic *mania* that the dialogues have as their ultimate content.

In all reading, however, it is necessary to begin at the surface
and work toward what lies beneath. To use the more visceral
imagery Socrates often preferred, we must learn to be good
butchers and become skilled at cutting at the joints of the texts
(*Phaedrus* 265e). How to begin? I suggest that we use Homer's
Odyssey as a guide. If the meaning of the dialogues is comparable to Homeric Troy, buried and forgotten at Hisarlik, then
it is time to take up the books, read them seriously, and set to
work. More important than the figurative sense of my suggestion, however, is its literal sense. If the dialogues are Troy, the
best way to rediscover them is to take up the *Odyssey*, read it
seriously, and allow it to show us what to do. I am not propos-
ing yet another edifying comparative study. I am claiming that
Plato used the *Odyssey* consistently and purposefully as a key
source text for his most important dialogues. Searching out the
Homeric traces with the *Odyssey* in hand will uncover the foundations of their literary structure and better enable us to understand their meaning. If this seems academically scandalous, so
be it. The results of the search are all that matter.

Scholarly studies of Plato's use of sources in the dialogues
are generally too narrow and cautious. Their formal analyses
are based almost entirely on direct textual references such as
explicit quotations and obvious allusions. They consequently
have little concern for the significance of literary form and
structure. Studies searching for the meaning of Plato's dialogues, on the other hand, are usually far too sweeping and
incautious, tending toward broad generalities. Recently, the
attempt to combine the formal narrowness of philology and
the abandon of speculative interpretation has become quite a

reputable scholarly enterprise.[5] This is not what I have in mind. In the *Phaedrus*, Plato has Socrates say that the formal analysis of a text is a study of the "logographic necessity" of its arrangement (264b). The arguments of some texts are easy to discover; the arguments of others are not. The latter should be praised for their "invention" as well as their arrangement (236a). I have in mind a study of the "inventive logographic necessity" of Plato's use of Homer.

The distance between Homer and Plato is not as great as those who perpetuate their antithetical "old quarrel" might believe, but neither is it as insignificant as many ancients imagined it to be. Plato does not allegorize Homer as many pre-Socratic philosophers, rhapsodes, and grammarians are thought to have done. It is quite likely that he wrote with such works at hand, but these texts—the documents of the "old quarrel" mentioned by Socrates—are lost to us. The ways in which his reading of Homer might have been influenced by such texts we cannot know with any certainty. However, from what we can know, it is possible to say that Plato uses Homer differently from those who preceded him in speculating about the deeper meaning of the epics. He certainly uses Homer differently from those who followed him historically, and even from those who allegorized Homer into a Platonist.[6] I do not intend to speculate about his use of the *Odyssey* in the dia-

5. My favorite study of Plato in this style is Jacques Derrida, "Plato's Pharmacy," in *Dissemination*, trans. B. Johnson (Chicago: University of Chicago Press, 1981), 61–171. A more temperate and philologically interesting study of the "mixed mode" of Plato's dialogues, based on Bakhtin's notion of intertextuality, is Andrea Nightingale, *Genres in Dialogue: Plato and the Construct of Philosophy* (Cambridge: Cambridge University Press, 1995). See also Stephen Halliwell, *The Aesthetics of Mimesis: Ancient Texts and Modern Problems* (Princeton: Princeton University Press, 2002), 37–150. Halliwell argues that Plato was a "romantic puritan" with a "profoundly ambivalent" attitude toward art and poetry (26).

6. Neoplatonic allegorizations of Homer are discussed by Robert Lamberton, *Homer the Theologian: Neoplatonist Allegorical Reading and the Growth of the Epic Tradition* (Berkeley and Los Angeles: University of California Press, 1986); and J. Pépin, "The Platonic and Christian Ulysses," in *Neoplatonism and Christian Thought*, ed. D. J. O'Meara (Norfolk: International Society for Neoplatonic Studies, 1982), 3–18.

logues after the manner of the Patristic apologists, Philo, or pseudo-Heraclitus. It is the significance of his deliberate use of the *Odyssey* as a source text that is of primary interest to me.

In contemporary literary criticism, there are any number of studies comparing texts with one another in general terms, situating them in encompassing cultures or traditions, noting similar formal patterns, and speculating broadly about ambiguous influences.[7] Such studies do not address the questions raised by an author's deliberate use of source texts. There are, of course, also any number of scholarly studies concerned with establishing sources for a given text by cataloging direct quotations and allusions.[8] In Western society, a list of the most frequently cited classic texts would include Plato's dialogues, even if at some distance behind the Bible and Shakespeare's plays. Such books are foundational for our civilization and culture. However, despite their importance, or perhaps because of it, there are surprisingly few studies of the manner in which Plato, Shakespeare, and, say, the authors of the Gospels used source texts in their own writing.[9] Furthermore, there is little discussion of the topic as a whole that manages to avoid the unhelpful abstractions of current literary theory. There is not even a widely accepted name for the phenomenon. It is known variously as rewriting, rescripting, source work, text work, mime-

7. Several of the most famous are Erich Auerbach, *Scenes from the Drama of European Literature*, trans. R. Manheim (Minneapolis: University of Minnesota Press, 1981); Harold Bloom, *The Anxiety of Influence: A Theory of Poetry* (New York: Oxford University Press, 1973); and Northrop Frye, *The Great Code: The Bible As Literature* (New York: Harcourt, Brace, Jovanovich, 1982).

8. I have found J. LaBarbe, *L'Homère de Platon* (Liège: Faculté de Philosophie et Lettres, 1949), and Félix Buffière, *Les mythes d'Homère et la pensée grecque* (Paris: Société d'édition «Les Belles Lettres,» 1956), invaluable.

9. Recently, excellent studies have begun to appear. On biblical texts, for example, see Thomas L. Brodie, *The Quest for the Origin of John's Gospel* (New York: Oxford University Press, 1993) and *Genesis As Dialogue: A Literary, Historical, and Theological Commentary* (New York: Oxford University Press, 2001). On Augustine, see Robert McMahon, *Augustine's Prayerful Ascent: An Essay on the Literary Form of the "Confessions"* (Athens: University of Georgia Press, 1989). On Shakespeare, see E. Jones, *The Origins of Shakespeare* (Oxford: Clarendon, 1977); and Robert S. Miola, *Shakespeare's Reading* (New York: Oxford University Press, 2000).

sis, *imitatio*, rhetorical imitation, compositional genetics, intertextuality, and midrash. I will call it by one name, intentionally chosen for its lack of theoretical grounding: "refiguring." If an author uses a source text, deliberately and meaningfully, as part of a new text, the new text refigures the source. The parts of the source text an author refigures and the refigured parts of the new text can be discussed generally as literary tropes. My concern, therefore, is to understand the ways in which Plato's dialogues refigure the tropes of Homer's *Odyssey*.

The *Odyssey* is not the only source text used in composing the dialogues, but it is by far the most important. Plato may not have used it in the composition of all the dialogues, but its traces are evident in the most significant ones. His intent in refiguring the *Odyssey*, to put it simply, is to present Socrates as the greatest hero of Greece. Socrates is a new Odysseus, Athens is his Ithaca, and the episodes of Socrates' life—his divers encounters with sophists and philosophers, young men and compatriots—take on the aspect of dramatic events in Odysseus's wanderings and homecoming. It has always been a puzzle to determine the relation of Plato's dialogues. Computer analyses of grammatical usages have proved as unable to solve it as biographical and historical speculation or impressionistic thematic groupings of the texts. However, if the events described in many of the dialogues parallel episodes in the *Odyssey*, the poem serves as a template. One need only consider the manner in which Plato refigured the poem and distributed its parts across the dialogues to gain an insight into his understanding of their relation, no matter when they were written. And what is more, something of Plato's understanding of the *Odyssey* becomes clear along the way.

The history of interpretations of the *Odyssey* is a subject unto itself, and scholarly disagreements over the complexities of the epic's composition and form are sufficiently numerous that no brief account of its structure and substance will be entirely uncontroversial. My understanding of it is more controversial

than most. Over the years, I have read the *Odyssey* in several ways: at times, searching it for its "Platonic" traces; at
other times, without Plato in mind, driven back to it by reading what other scholars have made of it; and, in the best of
circumstances, for enjoyment alone. I have come to think that
it is far more important to understand Homer's poetry as the
culmination of traditions that were ancient even in the time
it was composed than it is to appreciate it as the foundation
of new literary traditions. The *Odyssey* has much in common
with the Mesopotamian *Epic of Gilgamesh*, for example. Both
are high cultural expressions of eastern Mediterranean civilizations about which we know very little, and both draw the
main features of their symbolism from even more archaic Near
Eastern cultures.[10] The origins of the symbolism are not inac-
cessible to us today, but we are not likely to discover much
about them through ethnography in the former Yugoslavia.[11]
The symbolism of the *Odyssey* has far more in common with
the practices of Siberian shamanism than it does with anything
sung at a never-ending south-Slavic wedding. I have been to
enough of the latter to be fairly confident of this opinion. The
former comparison requires some further explanation.

The dramatic events of Odysseus's travels, when arranged
chronologically, follow a pattern that outlines what might be
said to be Odysseus's initiation as a shaman. *Shamanism* is a
modern term describing the rites and symbols of certain mys-
tical practices common to tribal societies throughout the world.
Mircea Eliade's definitive study of the phenomenon provides
a fascinating catalog of its many forms, from Siberia and Tibet

10. See Cyrus H. Gordon, *Before the Bible: The Common Background of
Greek and Hebrew Civilizations* (New York: Harper and Row, 1962); and
Louis H. Feldman, "Homer and the Near East: The Rise of the Greek Ge-
nius," *Biblical Archaeologist* 59:1 (1996): 13–21.
11. See Milman Parry, *The Making of Homeric Verse: The Collected Pa-
pers of Milman Parry* (Oxford: Oxford University Press, 1971); Albert B.
Lord, *The Singer of Tales* (Cambridge: Cambridge University Press, 1960);
and M. W. M. Pope, "The Lord-Parry Theory of Homeric Composition,"
Acta Classica 6 (1963): 1–21. For a critical discussion, see Norman Austin,
Archery at the Dark of the Moon (Berkeley and Los Angeles: University of
California Press, 1975), 11–80.

to the Americas.[12] Although the particular manifestations can be quite varied, there are several characteristic features that appear across societies and historical epochs. To illustrate the relation of shamanism's "archaic techniques of ecstasy" and the poetic structure of the *Odyssey*, a brief summary will suffice.

Shamanism is the spiritual transformation of an initiate at the hands of various divinities—usually a male initiate and female divinities—by means of unusual rites, the most important of which are described in images of travel along the axis mundi. Shamans speak of world-trees, pillars, ladders, and the like; and underlying all such symbols is an experience of participation in a cosmic order the phenomenology of which is readily understandable to anyone who wonders at the night sky. As we see them, the heavens revolve around a still point, the top of the axis; the heavens are joined to the earth at an omphalos, a still point at which the axis touches the earth; and as the axis passes through the earth, it enters the underworld, the realm to which the bodies and souls of the dead descend. A shaman learns to travel along the axis mundi in both directions, down to the land of the dead and up through the spheres of the cosmos, and the events of his journey profoundly transform him. Again, such symbols have a readily understandable phenomenology: purification rituals and ecstatic experiences of participation in a transcendent order make the initiate more virtuous, we might

12. Mircea Eliade, *Shamanism: Archaic Techniques of Ecstasy*, trans. W. R. Trask (New York: Bollingen, 1964). In his concluding remarks, Eliade says: "[A] large number of epic 'subjects' or motifs, as well as many characters, images, and clichés of epic literature, are, finally, of ecstatic origin, in the sense that they were borrowed from the narratives of shamans describing their journeys and adventures in the superhuman worlds" (510). My arguments take up these suggestive insights. They also attempt to further Eric Voegelin's groundbreaking work in the symbolization of human experience in history. See "Equivalences of Experience and Symbolization in History," in *The Collected Works of Eric Voegelin, Volume 12, Published Essays, 1966–1985* (Columbia: University of Missouri Press, 1990), 115–33; and "The Symbolization of Order," in *Israel and Revelation*, vol. 1 of *Order and History* (Baton Rouge: Louisiana State University Press, 1956), 1–11. For my critical assessment of his work, see Zdravko Planinc, "The Significance of Plato's *Timaeus* and *Critias* in Eric Voegelin's Philosophy," in *Politics, Order, and History*, ed. G. Hughes, S. A. McKnight, and G. Price (Sheffield: Sheffield Academic Press, 2000), 327–75.

say, and certainly wiser about the mysteries of life and death. Consequently, on his homecoming, a shaman is recognized as a healer; in other words, his transformation makes him capable of curing the ills of others, of guiding their lives, and of providing a source of order for his society.

In Homer's hands, the compact tropes of shamanistic symbolism are differentiated and made remarkably subtle, and so much is added to the basic structure of the shaman's journey that it is almost obscured. Nevertheless, the core of the epic describing how Odysseus came to know many cities and minds, and how he had his homecoming and restored order on Ithaca, remains shamanistic. Homer's most significant alteration to the archaic symbolic structure is his augmentation of the series of travels along the axis mundi to places beyond the mortal realm with a complementary series of travels to societies that are beyond the societies of mortals. Odysseus's spiritual travels are bounded at one terminus of the axis mundi by Hades, from which he is returned with Teiresias's prophecy, and at the other by Zeus's celestial lightning bolt, which destroys his ship and begins his descent through the cosmos toward his homecoming. Within these ultimate bounds his more immediate and direct relations with lesser divinities are his erotic encounters with his guides, Circe and Calypso. And in the complementary series of travels with explicitly political significance, Odysseus discovers the extremes to which human societies might aspire through his encounters with the Cyclopes and the Phaeacians.

In Plato's hands, the tropes of Homer's epic are further differentiated, the original story is again made more subtle, a wealth of new material is incorporated, and the results of his extensive refiguring are distributed across many of the most important dialogues. Nevertheless, the core remains the same. In a previous book, *Plato's Political Philosophy*, I have argued that the *Republic* and the *Laws* are the most important parts of Plato's refiguring of Homer.[13] The two dialogues are not at odds, as is

---

13. Zdravko Planinc, *Plato's Political Philosophy: Prudence in the "Republic" and the "Laws"* (Columbia: University of Missouri Press, 1991). My work builds on the work of Barry Cooper, "'A Lump Bred Up in Dark-

commonly thought. The *Laws* complements the *Republic*, just as the second half of the *Odyssey* complements the first. In the *Republic*, the discussion of the nature of justice leads the interlocutors to consider parallels between types of souls and types of cities. From this basis, Plato develops his more explicit differentiation of the spiritual and political components of Odysseus's travels in a tale of Socrates' wanderings and homecoming that extends through several dialogues before coming to a conclusion in the *Laws*.

The spiritual component of Odysseus's travels is initially refigured in the *Republic* as Socrates' descent into the Hades of the Piraeus, where the discussion takes place, and his subsequent ascent in speech to a vision of the transcendent "good beyond being" (509b). The shamanistic imagery of psychic descents and ascents is repeatedly reformulated throughout the dialogue, most obviously in Socrates' concluding story in which a Pamphylian named Er returns from the dead and tells what he saw: the judgment of souls in the afterlife, the way in which

---

nesse': Two Tellurian Themes of the *Republic*," in *Politics, Philosophy, Writing: Plato's Art of Caring for Souls*, ed. Zdravko Planinc (Columbia: University of Missouri Press, 2000), 80–121. For a study of the significance of astronomy and cosmology in interpreting the symbolic forms of ancient myths, see Giorgio de Santillana and Hertha von Dechend, *Hamlet's Mill: An Essay on Myth and the Frame of Time* (Boston: Godine, 1977). For a comparable study of Homer, see the papers of Edna Florence Leigh, in *Homer's Secret "Iliad": The Epic of the Night Skies Decoded*, comp. and ed. Florence Wood and Kenneth Wood (London: John Murray, 1999). Plato has been interpreted in similar spirit by Eva Brann in "The Music of the *Republic*," *Agon* 1 (1967): 1–117. Literary parallels between the works of Homer and Plato have also been noted by Charles P. Segal in "The Phaeacians and the Symbolism of Odysseus' Return," *Arion* 1:4 (1962): 17–64; and " 'The Myth Was Saved': Reflections on Homer and the Mythology of Plato's *Republic*," *Hermes* 106 (1978): 315–36; as well as by Robert Eisner in "Socrates As Hero," *Philosophy and Literature* 6 (1982): 106–18. For a discussion of the religious practices and interpretive traditions that likely influenced Plato's understanding of Homeric symbolism, see N. Grimaldi, "Le shamanisme socratique: Réflexion sur le langage dans la philosophie de Platon," *Revue de Métaphysique et de Morale* 73 (1968): 401–29; R. McGahey, *The Orphic Moment: Shaman to Poet-Thinker in Plato, Nietzsche, and Mallarmé* (Albany: SUNY Press, 1994), 27–50; and Peter Kingsley, *Ancient Philosophy, Mystery, and Magic: Empedocles and Pythagorean Tradition* (Oxford: Clarendon, 1995).

they choose new lives, and the manner of their rebirth by travel through the cosmos along the axis mundi.[14] Plato concludes the *Republic* by making the relation of Odysseus and Socrates quite explicit. In Socrates' recounting of Er's tale, the last to choose a new life is the soul of Odysseus. It chooses the life of a man who "minds his own business"; it chooses, in other words, the just life that Socrates himself claims to be living (*Republic* 620c). The story of Socrates' psychic ascent and subsequent acquisition of the virtues is frequently reformulated and retold in other di-

14. Arthur Platt rightly observes that "modern commentators are as much in the dark about Er as were the ancients" ("Plato, *Republic* 614B," *Classical Review* 25 [1911]: 13). The best manuscripts of the *Republic*, the oldest of which dates to the ninth century C.E., agree on the only passage in which the name is given: Ἡρὸς τοῦ Ἀρμενίου, τὸ γένος Παμφύλου (614b). However, Gerard Boter warns that even the agreement of the most reliable primary manuscripts and the indirect tradition of references in other ancient texts should not lead us into "flattering ourselves with the conviction" that we have "what Plato wrote"; such agreement might be due to earlier "contamination" (*The Textual Tradition of Plato's "Republic"* [Leiden: E. J. Brill, 1989], 79). The ancient commentators found much to speculate about in this passage. At the end of the first century C.E., Plutarch read the patronymic as Ἀρμενίου ("Harmonious"), interpreting the character symbolically (*Symposiakon* 9.740b). In the following century, Clement identified him with Zoroaster in the context of an argument that Plato's writings took their best insights from Hebrew Scripture (*Stromata* 5.103). In the tenth or eleventh century C.E., the *Suda Lexicon*, following Proclus's prosaic reading (*Commentary on the Republic*, ad loc), standardized the name of the man as Er in the nominative case, but it did so while identifying him as the Hebrew Er, the brother of Onan (Gen. 38:3–4; Luke 3:28). The point of such identification is to subsume Plato's work in a narrative that diminishes all things before the Christian revelation; and, in this instance, the lack in Plato is hinted to be a limited and defective eros, inferior to universal Christian *caritas*. Modern commentators follow the tradition of referring to the man as Er, but without any concern to interpret the character's literary or symbolic significance. They are now more concerned with the patronymic. James Adam argues that "τοῦ Ἀρμενίου is of course 'son of Armenius,' not 'the Armenian'" (*The "Republic" of Plato* [Cambridge: Cambridge University Press, 1902], ad loc). Platt claims, on the contrary, that the name is Armenian, and that "Ἡρὸς τοῦ Ἀρμενίου means 'Ara the son of Aram'" ("Plato, *Republic* 614B," 14). The ancient and modern commentators alike give no notice to the fact that Plato deliberately gives the man who returns from the dead to tell the saving tale a name that, in its genitive case (Ἡρὸς), is similar to that of the divinity Eros (Ἔρως). Socrates' recollection of Er's recollection of Hades is thus a tale the symbolic structure of which is halfway between an archaic tale of a

alogues. In the *Symposium*, for example, Socrates' account of his initiation in the mysteries of "erotics" *(erōtika)* by Diotima, the Mantinean prophetess, follows the same form: the ascent of the "rising steps" of the ladder of love toward the "perfect revelations" ends with one being "astounded" or "undone" *(ekpeplēxai)* by the vision of the highest things (209e–212a), as Odysseus was undone when his ship was struck and destroyed by Zeus's lightning bolt at the zenith of his journey (*Odyssey* 12.403–19).

The political component of Odysseus's omphallic travels also appears in many of the dialogues. Every depiction of Athens divided between the power of sophists and tyrannical politicians, on the one hand, and the authority of Socrates, on the other, recalls the situation of Ithaca, torn between the lawlessness and barbarism of the suitors, whose society is little better than that of the Cyclopes, and the authority of Odysseus, returned with hidden gifts from the glorious society of the Phaeacians. Odysseus returns with the equivalent of the powers of a shaman, and in being recognized he restores order to his realm. In the *Gorgias*, Plato has Socrates announce his similar authority in the shocking, and indeed revolutionary, statement that he is the only living Athenian able to "practice politics," the only one with "the true political art" (521d). However, Athens does not recognize him, even when it learns that his authority is omphallic, sanctioned by the oracle at Delphi (*Apology* 21a). The glories of the perfectly just city he has seen remain hidden within him. Odysseus made Ithaca resemble the heavenly city of the Phaeacians, but at great cost. Socrates' virtues are greater: he has overcome Odysseus's last vice, the love of honor (*Republic* 620c). Consequently, he says that the heavenly city is to be founded only within one's own soul (592a–b).

The *Republic* includes a complete description of the spiritual component of Socrates' omphallic travels, but an incomplete description of the political component. The dialogue's parallel

---

shaman guiding a dead soul along the axis mundi to Hades and returning to tell what he saw and Plato's more extensive accounts of the erotic and daimonic quality of Socrates' anamnetic philosophy.

account of types of souls and types of cities is not parallel at all levels: Socrates' vision of the "good beyond being" is not fully developed as a city in speech. In the *Odyssey*, both components are present: after Zeus's lightning bolt ends his ascent, Odysseus spends seven years trapped with Calypso, and then travels to the land of the Phaeacians, the best regime. The city in speech of the *Republic* is not comparable to the heavenly Phaeacian city. Plato has Socrates ironically name it the "beautiful city," the *kallipolis* (527c)—the polis of Calypso, as it were. Furthermore, Plato indicates that the political discussion of the dialogue is incomplete by refiguring the episode of Odysseus's departure from Calypso's island in the famous symbol of the argument's "three waves," the final one of which is the rule of philosopher-kings. The *kallipolis* of the *Republic* has its place in the give-and-take of the discussion, but Socrates leaves it behind when he strikes out to reach the perfectly just and good city, ruled by true philosophers. It is only in the *Laws* that Socrates, in the literary disguise of the Athenian Stranger, finds the Phaeacian city.

Throughout the history of political philosophy, from Cicero to the present, it has been a commonplace to assume that the *Republic* is a statement of Plato's highest political ideal. The *Laws* has been entirely forgotten, or considered spurious, or thought to be the work of a cranky old man; and when it has been studied seriously, Magnesia, its city in speech, has always been understood as inferior to the *Republic*'s "beautiful city." However, when the dialogues are read with the *Odyssey* open beside them, their relation appears in an entirely different light. In composing the *Republic*, Plato already had the *Laws* in mind; and Magnesia is a higher ideal than the *kallipolis*. Plato's political philosophy is not what the majority of his Roman, Christian, and modern readers have understood it to be.

There is a great deal yet to be learned about Plato's dialogues. The archaeological dig, using the *Odyssey* as map and guide, has only begun to break ground. Each initial discovery, even if its place in the whole is not clear, confirms that this is the place to dig, and that, in time, the order of the fascinating things being unearthed will become evident to us. The present study is

more digging in adjacent areas. It continues my work on the literary and substantive continuities of the *Republic* and *Laws* by
examining Homeric imagery in the *Phaedrus* and the *Timaeus*
and *Critias*. My intent is to use the study of refigured Homeric
tropes in these dialogues to understand them better individually and in relation to Plato's other major works. Scholarly
questions will be raised and addressed, because books should
be contributions to knowledge. But I am not drawn by scholarship as an end in itself; the far richer implications of such
a research project attract me. By reading the dialogues in this
way, Plato becomes familiar to us; and through him, Homer;
and through the literary expression of their friendship, a living
sense of the best of Greek culture.

The *Phaedrus* and the *Timaeus* and *Critias* are almost always
discussed in a topical manner. The *Timaeus* has been picked
through for its theological or scientific doctrines for millennia.
Its companion dialogue, the *Critias,* is seldom read, and then
only to be reduced to its Atlantis story or puzzled over because
of its ostensible incompleteness. The *Phaedrus* has recently en-
joyed a good deal of academic attention because of its exotic
nature: parallels have been seen to modern understandings of
erotics and literary theory, and sometimes both together. However, the cosmology of the *Phaedrus* seems so different from
the one in the *Timaeus* that the question of their relation is almost never raised. When the dialogues are considered together,
it is usually in the context of interpretive schemes primarily
concerned with distinguishing periods in the development of
Plato's metaphysical doctrines. There are no studies that treat
these dialogues—in the full range of the many intriguing things
they present—as a coherent, unified group of works with a
well-defined relation to Plato's other major dialogues.

I will argue that the main literary features of the *Phaedrus,*
Timaeus, and *Critias* are taken from the books of the *Odyssey*
that tell the story of Odysseus's stay with the Phaeacians immediately before his homecoming. When Odysseus swims to
shore on Scheria, the island of the Phaeacians, he encounters
Nausicaa, the king's daughter. Even before revealing his iden-
tity to the royal court, Odysseus is well received as a guest:

there are songs sung in his honor by the poet Demodocus, several of which recount the Trojan War; there are athletic contests in which he competes; and his request for passage to Ithaca aboard one of the Phaeacians' magical ships is graciously granted. When Demodocus's songs make it impossible for Odysseus to avoid telling the Phaeacians who he is, he takes the place of the poet and tells them the story of his earlier travels from Troy to Calypso's island, by way of Hades, and the terrible passage between Skylla and Charybdis. They listen, amazed, and then send him on his way with great and numberless gifts. Odysseus wakes from a gentle sleep on an Ithacan beach. The ship that brought him is destroyed by Poseidon, who, in his anger against the Phaeacians for aiding Odysseus, turns on them, intent on destroying their city as well.

Plato breaks up the sequence of tropes of this lovely episode and uses different parts for different dialogues. In the *Phaedrus*, Odysseus's encounter with Nausicaa on the shore of Scheria is refigured in Socrates' encounter with Phaedrus by the river Ilissus outside the walls of Athens. This provides a basic structure for the text, upon which Plato builds. The concluding prayer of the *Phaedrus* echoes the circumstances of Odysseus's waking on the shores of Ithaca, and the events between his arrival on Scheria and his homecoming are reworked in the substantive core of the dialogue. Most significantly, in Socrates' second speech in praise of Eros—known as the "palinode" because it retraces the steps of his first speech and recants its unintentional blasphemies—Plato combines the shamanistic or omphallic aspects of Odysseus's encounter with Nausicaa with comparable imagery from the later tale of Odysseus's voyages, primarily the episodes describing his relations with female immortals or semidivinities—Calypso, Circe, the Sirens— and with the ever watchful Athena. The marvelous result of Plato's refiguring, especially the palinode's grand vision of the ascent of souls through the cosmos to its roof to behold the hyperouranian region, is one of the best expressions in the dialogues of the unity of the music *mania* of poetry and the erotic *mania* of philosophy.

The *Timaeus* and *Critias* should be read together as one work, the dramatic structure of which is based on scenes of Odysseus's time at the Phaeacian court. Demodocus sings three songs for Odysseus. The first and the third tell of the Trojan War, and the sufferings they recount move the silent Odysseus to grief. The second, sung at the contests, is a celebratory tale of Aphrodite's affair with Ares. Plato refigures these tropes, in sequence, as the three speeches made by Critias and Timaeus; and Socrates' largely silent reactions to them can be inferred from the effects of Demodocus's songs on Odysseus. Plato uses Demodocus's song of Ares and Aphrodite as the basis for his presentation of the main features of Timaeus's Pythagorean cosmology. It is likely that he worked with Pythagorean interpretations of the *Odyssey* while composing the dialogue, but the traces of Homer's text are sufficiently clear without the lost mediating texts. Plato uses Demodocus's songs of the Trojan War as the basic structure for his presentation of Critias's tale of the ancient war between Athens and Atlantis. Many of the puzzling details of the story have their origins in the *Odyssey*: for example, the submerging of Atlantis recalls Poseidon's destruction of Scheria. But, more important, the Homeric subtext of the dialogue gives an indication of why it ends so abruptly. The *Critias* is not unintentionally incomplete. Demodocus's song was dramatically interrupted by Odysseus's weeping; he then revealed his name to the Phaeacians and took the place of the poet. In similar fashion, Critias's sophistic story is dramatically interrupted; and it is surpassed by a better story, told in other dialogues.

None of Plato's dialogues is complete in the sense of being a self-sufficient work; they all point to other dialogues. The *Timaeus* and *Critias* pair is not unfinished, but it is incomplete in that Plato deliberately does not present his best understanding of politics and cosmology there. The Homeric traces in the dialogues are often the best indications of where one should turn when something seems lacking. Plato's cosmology, for instance: the lacks of the *Timaeus* have traditionally been considered definitive of "Platonism" and filled in with biblical theology. However, a study of the Homeric tropes of the dialogues leads one from the *Timaeus* to the *Phaedrus*. The tropes on which the Pythagorean account of the *Timaeus* is based are enveloped by the tropes on which the *Phaedrus* is based. What is more, Plato uses the same trope of Odysseus's relation to Demodocus in presenting the cosmological account of both dialogues, thus indicating quite clearly his understanding of the superiority of Socrates' erotics to Timaeus's Pythagorean mechanics. The *Phaedrus* is incomplete as well. It looks to the *Republic,* as do the *Timaeus* and *Critias.* And even the most celebrated and apparently self-sufficient of the dialogues, the *Republic,* is incomplete. The many things discussed by Socrates and his interlocutors that night he "went down" to Piraeus can be followed up in different ways. The *Timaeus* and *Critias* continue the argument in one direction. They mark the road not taken by Plato's Socrates. The *Phaedrus* marks the higher, longer way from the *Republic* to the *Laws.*

Descent

The *Timaeus* and *Critias*

Until recently, it had been traditional to assume that Plato intended the *Timaeus* and *Critias* as parts of a sequence of dialogues beginning with the *Republic*. The best evidence for this reading is the relation of the dialogues' settings. The *Republic* opens with Socrates recounting the discussions of the previous night, from memory, for an unnamed auditor. The *Timaeus* opens with the news that there had been four people listening to Socrates' recitation that day, not one, and that they have met again to speak further of such matters. Socrates appears with Timaeus, Critias, and Hermocrates; the fourth person present yesterday—again unnamed—is unaccountably missing. The temporal continuity of the dialogues had always been thought to be self-evident, but nothing was ever made of it. The tradition of reading Plato's dialogues as treatises on meta-physics, cosmology, logic, and the like, written in an attractive but dispensable literary form, began in the schools of philosophy shortly after Plato's death.

Recently, on the basis of a philological quibble or two and speculation about Plato's genealogy, it has become the norm for scholars to deny that Plato intended these dialogues to have any temporal or literary continuity. The new orthodoxy on their relative dramatic dates, like the one it displaced, has no consequence for interpreting the doctrines thought to be presented in the dialogues: Plato's theories on this or that topic are best understood, it is claimed, by attending primarily to the historical dates of the dialogues' composition. The new ortho-doxy changes little, but it does have the ironic consequence of making the dialogues less historically interesting. It had been traditional to identify the Critias of these dialogues as Plato's uncle, Critias the tyrant, though he had been considered as little more than a cipher for an odd tale Plato wished to tell but did not complete. Scholars now identify him as the grandfather of the tyrant, unknown except for the fact that his name was also Critias: on the whole, perhaps a more fitting character to associate with the telling of a very old and somewhat pointless story, but far less intriguing.[1]

The traditional view of the dialogues as a trilogy is, I think, the right one, but it is wrong to ignore the literary features of Plato's works in a search for his doctrines. The temporal and dramatic continuities of the dialogues, seen in light of the Homeric tropes used by Plato in their composition, are the best indications of how Plato intended the accounts of cosmology and politics given by Timaeus and Critias to be understood. Timaeus presents his own understanding in the dialogue, not a "Platonic" one. He is a Pythagorean from Locris in Italy. Al-though it is likely that Plato constructed Timaeus's account from contemporary Pythagorean texts, the extent to which he does or does not agree with anything said in it can be deter-

---

1. The debate is summarized in Warman Welliver, *Character, Plot, and Thought in Plato's "Timaeus"-"Critias"* (Leiden: E. J. Brill, 1977), 50–57.

mined only from the literary form of the story he uses to present it. And Critias is indeed Plato's uncle, the puzzling man who wrote a prodigious number of books and plays before satisfying his political ambitions by becoming one of the murderous Thirty Tyrants. Even though few fragments of Critias's own works survive for comparison, it is evident that the tale of the war between Atlantis and Athens is a sophist's story. Plato made his uncle a major character in the *Timaeus* and *Critias* not from an abiding "respect and affection,"[2] but rather to show up the stark contrast between a sophist and tyrant, on the one hand, and a true philosopher, on the other. The poetry of the dialogues, no matter when they were written, best illuminates their philosophic content; and the poetry of the *Timaeus* and *Critias*, the main features of which are refigured from episodes of Odysseus's stay with the Phaeacians, best reveals the contrast between Plato's love of Socrates and his open disdain for Critias.

The continuity of the dialogues' dramatic settings is much less difficult to determine than their likely dramatic dates. Plato did not write histories. The events of the dialogues are historically plausible, in the style of many modern novels, but no more. And our knowledge of ancient Greece is far too spotty for us to have the tacit familiarity necessary to interpret Plato's literary-historical references confidently and in the detail that the subtlety of his writing requires. We cannot be certain of the year, month, and specific days Plato intended for the setting of the *Republic, Timaeus,* and *Critias,* and given what we do know about the period it is doubtful that we will ever have anything better than a good guess. Even worse: there is a snarl of philological riddles around the question of dramatic dating that no guess will untangle successfully.

In what year is the trilogy set? The *Republic* (368a) mentions a battle of Megara in which Glaucon and Adeimantus, Plato's brothers, recently fought, but is it the one in 424 or 409? The dialogue takes place in the home of Cephalus, the Syracusan arms

2. W. K. C. Guthrie, *The Sophists* (Cambridge: Cambridge University Press, 1971), 299.

dealer, but when did he and his sons all reside in the Piraeus? And was Cephalus even alive when his sons, Polemarchus, Euthydemus, and Lysias, were mature enough to participate in debates with Socrates? The *Timaeus* and *Critias* are dated according to which Critias is thought to be intended: a difference of two generations. But what of Hermocrates? When was the Sicilian tyrant ever in Athens? And for what reason? If these are not problems enough, there is a further troubling question: in what week is the trilogy set? The *Republic* occurs during a festival for the goddess Bendis, thought to take place in mid-Thargelion (the month spanning late May and early June). The *Timaeus* and *Critias* occur during a festival for "the goddess" (*Timaeus* 21a), but which goddess is meant? The largest in honor of Athena, usually signified by such a passing remark, is the Panathenaia at the end of Hekatombaion (July–August), far too late to be possible. And then there are the problems of the sources available to assist us in puzzling through these matters. The relevant ones are few: Thucydides' *Peloponnesian War*, Xenophon's *Hellenica*, and Lysias's *Orations* are contemporary; Diodorus's *History* and Plutarch's *Lives* are later. Each is reliable, but on these questions the evidence is scant and sometimes contradictory.

None of the possible dates suggests uncontroversial answers to all of these interpretive questions. How then to determine which is a best guess? Since Plato is a brilliant writer, I think it is necessary, above all, to consider which date would make the dialogues most interesting. Using this criterion, there is only one contender: the week of the Bendideia and Plynteria in 407.[3] The date is historically plausible, in a literary way, and several of its implications are rather intriguing.

By 407, Glaucon and Adeimantus, at suitable ages, have distinguished themselves in the Athenian victory at Megara in 409—the battle of 424 was an indifferent draw—and enough time has passed for Glaucon's lover to have written and cir-

---

3. According to our best estimates, the Bendideia took place circa 19 Thargelion; the Plynteria, within a week, circa 25 Thargelion. This is the week accepted by A. E. Taylor, *A Commentary on Plato's "Timaeus"* (Oxford: Clarendon, 1927), note on *Timaeus* 17a1.

culated a poem about their courage.[4] Cephalus's business is thriving during the latter stages of the Peloponnesian War, and Lysias has been home in the Piraeus since 411 after having spent several decades in Italy. However, Cephalus himself has been dead for many years. Perhaps this explains why Plato has Socrates say that Cephalus looks very old, and that he is surprised even to see him there (328b). Cephalus's fleeting, ghostly presence in the first book of the dialogue, welcoming Socrates to Piraeus, is partly Plato's refiguring of a famous Homeric trope: the intrepid arrival of Odysseus in Hades, where he is astonished to be greeted by the soul of Elpenor, who he had thought was still alive.[5] Cephalus's son Polemarchus, named "Warlord" by his father, would soon join him in death. In three years, Athens would finally be defeated by Sparta, and the oligarchic regime subsequently established to rule Athens, the regime of the Thirty Tyrants, would execute him. In 407, however, the outcome of the war is still uncertain. Even Critias, who would soon become one of the Thirty loyal to Sparta, still has hopes of an Athenian victory.

Critias publicly supported the recall from exile of his friend Alcibiades,[6] whom he thought the only person fit to lead the Athenian military forces. Although Alcibiades had fled to Sparta when the Athenians recalled him for trial during the

4. I have learned from James Rhodes that there is further evidence for a late date. In his book, *Eros, Wisdom, and Silence: Plato's Erotic Dialogues* (Columbia: University of Missouri Press, 2003), he makes a convincing case that the *Republic* is set in the period 408–405 by comparing Plato's several references to Theages. He points out that in the *Theages,* Socrates mentions that a campaign against Ephesus and Ionia, which we know to have been fought in 409, is currently under way. At the end of the dialogue, Socrates agrees to admit Theages, then healthy and aspiring to a political career, to his company as a probationary student. In the *Republic,* however, Socrates refers to Theages as a present comrade whose sickness prevents him from abandoning philosophy for politics (496b–c). It is quite reasonable to conclude, therefore, that the *Republic* is set circa 408–405.

5. There are ancient readings recognizing that Cephalus was long dead at the dramatic date of the *Republic*. See Bernard Bosanquet, *A Companion to Plato's "Republic,"* 2d ed. (London: Methuen, 1895), 38; and Brann, "The Music of the *Republic*," 3.

6. The nature of their relationship is most clearly evident in Plato's *Protagoras* and Xenophon's *Memorabilia* (1.2.12–38).

disastrous Sicilian campaign, he was believed to have surrep-
titiously aided the Athenian cause while there; and when he
later fled Sparta for the Persian court, the Athenians considered
forgiving him his crimes. After the Athenian navy won several
battles in the Hellespont under his leadership while still in exile, they were convinced of his loyalty. Alcibiades sailed into the
Piraeus during the festival of Plynteria in 407, and the people of
Athens all stopped what they were doing to celebrate his ominous return. Democrats and oligarchs alike loved Alcibiades,
or thought him useful, although for different reasons; and he, in
turn, did not think it necessary to distinguish between paths to
power. On the day of his return, all differences were put aside
in a collective anticipation of imminent victory.

Hermocrates, the Sicilian tyrant who had defeated the Athenian expedition, had had a similarly unstable career. A democratic coup during an absence from Syracuse resulted in his
exile in 409, and he too ended up in Persia, in the company of
Spartan ambassadors to the court of Pharnabazos. In the spring
of 407, his whereabouts are uncertain: he was likely returning
from Persia, planning a reconquest of Syracuse, and looking
for support in all quarters. Critias would have found him a
companionable houseguest. When Hermocrates did eventually return to Sicily with his own forces, Sicilian politics being
what they are, he was slain before he had consolidated power.
In 405, his son-in-law Dionysius succeeded in becoming tyrant.
Dionysius's eldest son by his second marriage, also named
Dionysius, and Dion, his son-in-law by yet another marriage,
were to become very familiar to Plato. The *Seventh Letter* tells
the story of Plato's several trips to Sicily in futile attempts to
educate the younger Dionysius and advise his friend Dion on
the difficulties of attempting to reform corrupt polities.

If the *Republic*, *Timaeus*, and *Critias* are set in 407, during the
week of the Plynteria, the circumstances are palpably tense.
Strongly held convictions of political and military conquest
cloud the reality of Athens's impending collapse. The democrats of Cephalus's household in the Piraeus, with whom Socrates debates the nature of justice in the *Republic*, tend toward
the tyrannical understanding of politics advocated by their

guest, the sophist Thrasymachus. The guests of Critias's household in Athens, with whom Socrates meets in the *Timaeus*, tend
toward the understanding of politics advocated by their oligarchic and sophistic host.[7] In the end, all political differences
are put aside: the city empties when the Athenians rush to the
harbor to welcome Alcibiades; all decisions against him are
reversed, and he is given complete power. They ignore everything Socrates has told them about politics, about philosophy,
and about their dangerous love of Alcibiades. They ignore the
auspices as well. The Plynteria was the most ancient festival of
the goddess, during which the clothes of the Athena Polias—a
far more important religious icon than the Athena Parthenos—
were taken to be washed ritually in the Aegean. The day the
statue of the city's protective goddess stood veiled during the
washing of her garment was thought to be unpropitious for
the undertaking of any important venture.[8]

  Socrates' descent to the Piraeus, begun in the *Republic*, ends
in the *Timaeus* and *Critias*. On the day of the Plynteria, Socrates stands in for the goddess. Plato has Socrates uncharac-
teristically call attention to his unusually fresh, festive clothes
(*Timaeus* 20c). Critias politely ignores him and tells a story that
he thinks is a fitting tribute to the goddess: an archaic tale of
the submersion of ancient Athens, told on the day of one of the

---

7. Hermocrates serves well as a symbol of Critias's emerging ambitions, as an allusion to the imminent defeat of Alcibiades' "Athenian expedition," and as a warning for Plato's Sicilian friends. The *Timaeus* and
Critias were likely written when Dion's own political ambitions were at
their greatest. Critias's story of the war between Athens and Atlantis has
some relevance for the contemporary political circumstances in Syracuse,
and Plato's dramatic use of Hermocrates as a character in the dialogues
is likely intended to remind Dion and his friends of discussions of sordid
Sicilian politics they had had in person. Dion succeeded in taking power
briefly, through force of arms, but was assassinated in 353. Plato's subsequent advice to Dion's friends, once again counseling prudence, is given
in the *Seventh Letter*.
  8. There is uncertainty and disagreement even about these basic features of the festival. It is possible that the statue was also carried to the
sea and washed. See L. R. Farnell, *The Cults of the Greek States* (Oxford:
Clarendon Press, 1896), 1:261–63; and C. J. Herington, *Athena Parthenos
and Athena Polias: A Study in the Religion of Periclean Athens* (Manchester:
Manchester University Press, 1955), 8–12, 28–30.

city's most archaic festivals, the submersion of Athena Polias, as it were. He says it is a true story, passed down verbatim through the millennia to his report of it. But the tale is completely invented. It is a dazzling display of sophistic rhetoric suited to the occasion and the audience. Its only truth is the political ambition Critias cannot entirely hide under a thin veil of readily decipherable allegory. The *Critias* seems to be unfinished, but Plato deliberately cuts it off at its most dramatic moment. Critias, in full rhetorical flight, is about to utter a blasphemy—a contrived speech by Zeus before the assembly of the gods—when word of Alcibiades' return reaches him, and he no longer feels the desire to play the intellectual.[9]

The ritual of the covering and uncovering *(katakalypsis, apokalypsis)* of the Athena Polias during the washing of her *peplos* has a literary parallel in the covering and uncovering of Athena's favorite hero in the *Odyssey*. When Odysseus reaches the shores of Ogygia, Calypso's island, the goddess gives him new clothing and warm hospitality. For seven years, Odysseus is hidden from the mortal realm by Calypso, "she who conceals" *(kalyptō)*, until Athena's intervention with Zeus brings about his release *(Odyssey* 5). And when Odysseus later washes up, naked, on the shore of Scheria, he is given new clothing by the godlike Nausicaa. His reception at the court of the Phaeacians is most generous, but Odysseus covers *(kalypse*, 8.85) his face with his cloak, weeping and lamenting, when Demodocus begins to sing of the battles at Troy.

9. Plato's abrupt conclusion for the *Timaeus-Critias* has a literary precedent in Aristophanes' *Frogs*, first performed in Athens during the time of Alcibiades' return. The comedy is set in Hades, and involves a contest between Aeschylus and Euripides, judged by the god Dionysos. Their rather prolonged verbal sparring threatens to end in a draw, but Dionysos settles the question of which of them will be returned to life by asking them their opinion of Alcibiades (1418–34). For a comparison of the last scene of the *Frogs* and Xenophon's description of Alcibiades' dramatic return to Athens, see David Gribble, *Alcibiades and Athens: A Study in Literary Presentation* (Oxford: Clarendon, 1999), 118.

Plato's refiguring of the *Odyssey* in the *Republic* and subsequent dialogues develops the parallel between the Homeric episodes and the Athenian festival. In the *Republic,* Socrates' discussion of justice in the cities and minds of men moves toward the best regime and the highest revelations. The political discussion remains trapped by the premises of the *kallipolis;* it only touches on the first premise of the best regime—the rule of philosopher-kings—as Odysseus only grasped a rock in desperation when a great wave carried him toward the shores of Scheria (*Republic* 473c–e; *Odyssey* 5.424–37). The psychological discussion, in contrast, reaches its end: Plato presents the various aspects of Socrates' revelatory account of the "good beyond being" in three images—the sun, the divided line, and the ascent from the cave—that are based on episodes from the tale Odysseus tells the Phaeacians after coming ashore on Scheria.

The same episodes are refigured differently in the *Phaedrus* and the *Timaeus* and *Critias.* In the *Timaeus* and *Critias,* the descent begun in the *Republic* continues: Homer's vivid depictions of Odysseus's reactions to Demodocus's songs are the basis for Plato's presentation of the vast differences between Socratic erotics and the cosmology and politics of Timaeus and Critias. And the dialogues are framed by references to the Plynteria that emphasize the imminent end to the military and political decline of Athens, on the one hand, and the brilliant alternative of Socrates, on the other, completely ignored by Athenians on the day he was dressed in festive garb, a symbol of political and spiritual renewal. In the *Phaedrus,* the ascent continues: Plato again refigures Odysseus's encounter with Nausicaa and the Phaeacian court to provide another account of the highest revelations. Socrates covers his head (*enkalypsamenos,* 237a) when he agrees to speak falsely in praise of a corrupt form of eros; when he recants in the palinode, however, he speaks with his head bare, and not covered in shame (*oukh . . . enkekalymmenos,* 243b). Socrates' final concealment and revelation are as the Athenian Stranger in the *Laws,* the dialogue in which he has a proper homecoming in a city in speech that escapes the tyrannical bonds of both contemporary Athenian politics and the garrison regime of the *kallipolis.* The *Laws* continues the ascent of the *Phaedrus*, as the *Critias* continues the descent of the *Timaeus*.

Plato's overlapping refigurations of the same symbols and episodes in the *Odyssey* not only provide a guide to understanding the literary and substantive relations of the dialogues; they also illuminate the complexity of Homer's poetic imagery. The story of the wanderings and homecoming of Odysseus is not a collection of colorful episodes; it is a subtly crafted tale in which each incident has its place in an account of the development of Odysseus's soul and the political consequences of his transformation. However, each episode is also more than a part of the aesthetic design; the more important ones serve as microcosms of the whole. The Phaeacians, for example: their city is the "best regime," an important station visited by Odysseus in Homer's densely patterned tale of his education in spiritual and political extremes that culminates in the restoration of justice on Ithaca; however, the Phaeacians are also a society unto themselves in which all the extremes are present and in conflict. Plato's refiguring of the books of the *Odyssey* depicting them is thus, in part, a differentiation of the several aspects of Homer's compact and overdetermined symbolism.

In the larger scheme of the *Odyssey*, the savage society of the Cyclopes and the godly society of the Phaeacians are the extremes to which human societies can aspire.[10] In the microcosm of the poetic episode, the extremes are stated together. The Phaeacians are said to have lived near the Cyclopes before they found their neighbors intolerable and migrated to Scheria (6.4–6). The members of the royal family—King Alcinous, Queen Arete, and their children—are the most godlike of the Phaeacians. However, the worst of the Phaeacians can be as insolent as the Cyclopes (6.262–84); and the tendency

10. The question of the relation between these two limiting societies and the human society of Ithaca is raised explicitly by the words Odysseus repeats—"Ah me, what are the people whose land I have come to this time, and are they violent and savage, and without justice, or hospitable to strangers, with a godly mind?"—when he first encounters the Cyclopes, and the Phaeacians, and then miraculously lands home again (*Odyssey* 6.119–21, 9.174–76, 13.200–202).

to such insolence even appears in the genealogy of the ruling family, most notably in Alcinous's own best-loved son, Laodamas (6.7–12, 7.48–77). When Odysseus is received at court, he is offered the seat of Laodamas, next to the king; he is also offered the hand of the princess Nausicaa (7.167–71, 311–14). Laodamas and his friend Euryalos are men "like murderous Ares himself"; they insult Odysseus publicly and challenge him to contests (8.115–17, 132–64). Nausicaa, in contrast, recognizes his worth and wishes he could be her husband (6.239–46). The Phaeacians are torn between the brutality of war-loving and the sublimity of eros, but the latter predominates. The very human tension in their loves also appears in the songs they enjoy hearing. Demodocus sings of the ruthless battles at Troy, and of the affair between Ares and Aphrodite. Again, the latter predominates: about Troy, Alcinous speaks poetically, saying that the gods bring about the destruction of peoples "for the sake of the singing of men hereafter" (8.579–80).

Homer presented conflict between the strongest aspirations in the souls of the best Phaeacians as a division in the lineage of the ruling household. The image must have had deep resonance with Plato. His family could trace a noble genealogy from the distant past, but since Solon's time the line had become divided: Critias now stood against Plato, the sophist against the philosopher, the lover of Alcibiades against the lover of Socrates, the tyrant against the just man. In the dialogues, Plato shows the consequences of this opposition for the men of his immediate family. As a promising youth, Charmides, Plato's uncle, comes under the sway of Critias: the *Charmides* shows him being turned against Socrates' virtuous influence. He eventually dies with Critias when the Thirty Tyrants fall. Glaucon and Adeimantus, Plato's brothers, are Socrates' main interlocutors in the *Republic:* they find the sophistry of Thrasymachus's tyrannical understanding of justice repugnant, but Glaucon, for one, allows his honor-loving and victory-loving to swell into a form of political idealism that prevents him from being able to follow Socrates' persuasion (cf. Xenophon, *Memorabilia* 3.6).

Lovers are caught up in the opposition as well. Plato's own

beloved, Dion of Syracuse, is part of Hermocrates' divided lineage. On his death, Hermocrates—the Sicilian Pericles, according to Thucydides—left his homeland polarized between the tyranny of Dionysius and the philosophical temper of Dion. As well, there is also Critias's beloved, Alcibiades, raised for rule by Pericles himself: in the *Symposium,* Plato steals him from Critias and makes him a lover of Socrates. Alcibiades confesses that his soul is deeply torn between love of power and love of Socrates (*Symposium* 215e–216c; cf. *Gorgias* 481c–482c). When Socrates is not present, however, the turmoil is less strongly felt; the love of the people is more satisfying. On the eventful day of the Plynteria in 407, Alcibiades does not seek out Socrates. Critias is there to welcome him home.

The opening of the *Republic* challenges a reader to recognize Socrates as his silent auditor does, as those with whom he discussed the nature of justice and the good failed to do. The opening of the *Timaeus* challenges a reader in the same way. What is the significance of his festive clothing on the day of the Plynteria? What does his summary of the previous day's discussion pass over? Why is he reticent to mention some things explicitly? And what must Socrates be thinking as Critias, his host, ostensibly attempts to honor him with his story and the discourse given by his houseguest Timaeus? Critias does not recognize Socrates, and Timaeus falls far short of the mark he sets for himself; however, Plato's poetic depiction of their failures is a lucid guide to understanding the nature and consequences of recognizing Socrates properly. The Homeric trope Plato refigures for the first word of the *Republic* puts the auditor and the reader in the place of Penelope, listening to Odysseus recount his travels. Her enduring love enables her to recognize and understand him. The Homeric tropes Plato refigures for the framing story of the *Timaeus* and *Critias* put the reader in the court of the Phaeacians. Critias responds to Socrates as Laodamas responds to Odysseus; his resentment at being displaced emerges as dismissive rudeness. And Timaeus sings as well as Demodocus; but Plato's Socrates, like Homer's Odysseus, tells a tale much better. The reader should see Socrates as Arete, Alcinous, and Nausicaa see Odysseus.

When Odysseus first appears at the Phaeacian court, he is wearing splendid clothing made by Queen Arete herself. Nausicaa had been washing her brothers' best clothes in a stream near the spot where Odysseus finally reached land, and when Odysseus surprised her with his supplication she offered him a mantle and tunic to cover his nakedness. Arete recognizes the clothes immediately, but discretely says nothing until she and the king are alone with Odysseus. She then asks the godlike stranger: "What man are you? and from whence? And who was it gave you this clothing?" (*Odyssey* 7.237–39). The circumstances are rather suggestive, and the questions require an equally discrete reply. During his telling of the tale of his escape from Calypso, Odysseus manages to explain how he came by the clothing without saying anything to compromise Nausicaa's virtue or reputation. He does not, however, identify himself. Only when Alcinous recognizes him—when his tears at Demodocus's song of the fall of Troy reveal who the stranger truly is—does he tell the Phaeacians his name (7.521–8.21).

In the *Timaeus* and *Critias*, Socrates does not seem a godlike stranger to his host and the other guests. Indeed, he is all too familiar—plain and undistinguished. There is surely no need for his host to ask him who he is. Socrates does on occasion identify himself in the dialogues, but usually not to those who do not ask him. In the *Gorgias*—the dialogue in which the beginning of philosophy is asking someone who he is (447c)—Plato has Socrates unexpectedly reveal himself to a disinclined audience as the only true statesman in Athens (521d), a declaration as dramatic and momentous as Odysseus's revelation of his name. In the *Timaeus*, however, Socrates sees no need to speak as openly to men of poor memory and little candor. Their day together begins pleasantly enough, and with some promise, but the discrete promptings he gives them in their recollections of the previous day's discourse are not taken up, and he slips into polite silence. These are not the men to assist him. Critias has offered his aid to another man he thinks godlike and in need of a homecoming: Alcibiades. Socrates is no one to him.[11]

Odysseus's response to Arete's questions emphasizes the difficulties of his escape, and only lesser divinities, Calypso and Poseidon, the ones who cause him suffering by hindering his journey, are mentioned by name. He says next to nothing about the assistance he received from higher divinities. There was Zeus's message compelling Calypso to release him; Leucothea's veil, which bore him up in the waves when his flimsy raft was destroyed by two great waves sent by Poseidon; and Zeus's calming of a river's flow to assist the weakened Odysseus coming ashore. In his telling of it, he seems the image of helplessness. When he describes how he entreated Nausicaa, he suggests nothing of the grace—a telling sign of the gods' favor—that attracted Nausicaa once she overcame her initial impression of his wildness. There would seem to be nothing erotic in their encounter at all. Nausicaa's innocence is uncompromised; her behavior toward a pitiable supplicant is blameless. And yet, the story puts Alcinous in mind of the erotic possibilities: he openly confesses his wish that this stranger might marry his only daughter.

At the beginning of the *Timaeus*, Plato refigures the trope of Odysseus's discrete reply as Socrates' odd summary of his previous day's narration of the *Republic*. Though Timaeus and Critias are both prepared to recite tales that evidently require prodigious feats of memory, Timaeus admits that he does not remember very well what Socrates said only yesterday (17b), and Critias's silence betrays a similar lack of attention to Socrates' words that his own story will make explicit. In recapping the "main points" (*kephalaion*, 17c) of the discussion, Socrates alters things to suit his audience. His summary emphasizes the literal sense of the suggestive imagery he and his interlocutors

11. According to Xenophon's report in the *Memorabilia* (1.2.24–39), Critias and Alcibiades, the most ambitious of the Athenians, often sought out Socrates in their youth, not because of his character or his way of life, but rather because they assumed that they could learn techniques of persuasive speech from him. As soon as they thought themselves ready for politics, they deserted his company.

had used in conversation. And it stops well short of the most significant parts of their discussion: the need for philosopher-kings, their education in the highest things, and the nature of their rule. It stops short, in other words, at the second wave of the argument concerning the *kallipolis*, mentioning nothing about the third wave and its consequences.[12] As Odysseus emphasizes the hindrances to his journey to Scheria, so Socrates emphasizes those features of the *kallipolis* that prevent the discussion from reaching a full understanding of the nature of justice and the good for human beings and cities. Timaeus, Critias, and Hermocrates are satisfied that they understand philosophy and politics well enough. The literal sense of the discussion of the *kallipolis* is, for them, a blueprint for a garrisoned city ruled by intellectuals, and although Socrates perhaps went on a bit in the telling of it, they think his remarks will serve adequately as a prelude for what they have to say on these topics.

Socrates drops a hint about what they have forgotten, but it is not picked up. He mentions the offspring of "the good" (19a), referring to the children of the best class of the regime, but also alluding to the image of the sun as the offspring of "the good itself" that began the discussion of philosophy proper (*Republic* 508b). No one says anything. He then asks his hosts explicitly if any important points have been left out. Timaeus replies that the summary is exactly what was said (19b).[13] And so, Socrates lets it go. The discussions of the *Republic* were quite animated and moved well beyond their initially limited

12. Compare Seth Benardete, "On Plato's *Timaeus* and Timaeus' Science Fiction," *Interpretation* 2:1 (1971): 22.

13. Scholars have disputed the question of the relation between the *Timaeus's* summary and the *Republic* for some time. R. G. Bury considers the summary an adequate recapitulation of the "political part" of the *Republic*: see *Plato in Twelve Volumes* (Cambridge: Harvard University Press, 1929), vol. 9, note to *Timaeus* 17c. Francis Cornford holds the diametrically opposed opinion: "There is, in fact, no part of the *Republic* of which it could be said that 'all the main points' were covered by the . . . summary." Therefore, he concludes, the *Timaeus* does not intend to refer to the *Republic* at all (*Plato's Cosmology* [1937; reprint, Indianapolis: Bobbs-Merrill, 1975], 11). Though contradictory, both views are consistent with the tradition of attempting to understand the "Platonism" of the *Republic* by way of the "Platonism" of the *Timaeus*.

understandings of political justice, but his hosts today recall only the static features of the *kallipolis*. If the summary did not put them in mind of the philosophical eros motivating the conversation, let them attempt to animate their recollections themselves. Take the *kallipolis*, he suggests, and set it in motion in the way you evidently prefer: show it at war (19b–20c). Critias and Hermocrates are quick to agree.

Timaeus should be the one to come to Socrates' assistance, but he too did not follow everything Socrates said yesterday. Much like Glaucon, who had refused to follow the highest flights of Socrates' erotic *mania*, dismissing his account of the good "beyond being" *(epekeina tēs ousias)* as ridiculous "daimonic hyperbole" (*Republic* 509b–c; cf. 533a), Timaeus counsels Socrates about the nature of philosophic inquiry: he claims that the lecture he will give is the best "likely story" *(eikota mython)* of the highest things, and snubs Socrates by adding that one "need not search beyond it" *(mēden eti pera zētein,* *Timaeus* 29d). For Timaeus, the story Socrates told yesterday, when he alleged to be reporting the warrior Er's tale *(apologon, Republic* 614b), was simply nonsense. The judgment of dead souls, ascent through the heavens and descent through the earth, souls choosing new lives before rebirth, the music of the heavenly spheres spinning on the axis mundi, divinities of various sorts everywhere—nothing but daimonic excess. Timaeus will speak of things as they are: physics, not fables.[14] The curl of his lip as he describes his speech as merely a "likely story" is easily discernible. But he would not smile if he understood the irony of Socrates' cutting reply. Socrates compliments the "prelude" of Timaeus's lecture and encourages him to go on to the "song" (*Timaeus* 29d), knowing that Timaeus did not understand and does not recall the account he gave yesterday of the three aspects of the education of true philosophers: the preparatory studies, or the "prelude"; the study of

14. Cornford observes that "the *Timaeus*, in contrast with the Myth of Er, says nothing about any music of the heavens," but the observation does not lead him to a clearer understanding of the distinction between "myth" and "science" in the dialogues than any of the other scholars he takes pains to correct (*Plato's Cosmology*, 79, 28–32).

dialectic, "the song itself" (*Republic* 531d); and the final vision of the good itself that enables them to order their lives and their cities (540a–b).[15] It is the last time Socrates speaks, save for once, politely, at the beginning of the *Critias* (108b). In the time it takes for Timaeus and Critias to tell their stories, it is not unlikely that Socrates occasionally regrets the absence of the one missing from their party, the man for whom he had been glad to recount the whole of the *Republic*.

The Phaeacians excel in athletic contests and dancing. The festivities in honor of Odysseus, following customs established by Zeus, celebrate both aspects of their character: their mastery of the skills necessary for war, demonstrated in their boxing, wrestling, and running, and their participation in the arts more suitable to times of peace, shown in their remarkable dancing. They are a perfect setting for Demodocus's song recounting the affair of Ares, god of war, and Aphrodite, goddess of love.

Demodocus sings wonderfully, and this is his most divine song, its beauty far surpassing his tales of conquest at Troy. However, Demodocus is only a minor character in Homer's transcending epic of Odysseus's wanderings and homecoming. Homer sings more wonderfully still. The story of Ares and Aphrodite has profound cosmological and philosophical implications. Demodocus's poetry uses images of the Olympians and their relations to express his meaning. Homer's poetry has greater subtlety. He too describes the Olympians; more significantly, though, he tells of the relation of human beings to the divinities, and of the ways in which human beings become godlike. The compact and overdetermined symbolism of earlier poetry is subsumed and differentiated in the epic imagery of the *Odyssey*. Homer sets Demodocus's song (8.266–366) in the

15. The differences between Socrates' and Timaeus's conceptions of philosophy are discussed by Scott R. Hemmenway, "Timaeus' Speech As Prologue to the Myth of Atlantis: Physics and Political Philosophy," a paper presented to the 1996 Annual Meeting of the American Political Science Association, San Francisco.

frame of a depiction, given in his own narrative voice, of inspiring Phaeacian dancing (8.256–65, 367–84): Odysseus is described as being held in awe and reverence (*sebas*, 8.384) by the dancers as they seem to leap into the sky to catch spheres falling from the clouds. A suggestion of the order of the cosmos, the ascent of dancers in attunement to its rhythm and harmony, the nature of contemplation: these few lines are sufficient to reveal how Homer's poetic symbolism surpasses the ancient songs. But there is more. The frame for Demodocus's song is encompassed in the story of the godlike Phaeacians; the storyteller of the Phaeacians is surpassed by Odysseus, telling the tale of his voyages; and the story of the Phaeacians itself is but one episode in Homer's song of Odysseus.[16]

Plato refigures Demodocus's song of Ares and Aphrodite in his presentation of Timaeus's Pythagorean cosmology. Timaeus is a character in Plato's tale of Socrates' life and death in the same way that Demodocus is a character in the *Odyssey*. Odysseus listens thoughtfully to Demodocus's song, but he also takes the poet's place and tells a better story. Demodocus's poetry is musical and elegant in its imagery. Odysseus speaks prosaically, and at some length; his depictions of divinities are rough-hewn; but the story of his travels is entirely captivating for the Phaeacians. Similarly, Socrates listens patiently to Timaeus's account, but Plato has him speak differently of the same things in other dialogues. Timaeus speaks of the cosmos with scientific rigor. Socrates seems to have less sophistication. In the *Symposium*, Alcibiades says Socrates' speeches are absurd and crude, always mentioning "pack-asses, blacksmiths,

---

16. In the extant fragments of the writings of Critias the tyrant, there is a tantalizing glimpse of the circumstances in which Plato composed the *Timaeus* and *Critias*. Critias is reported to have commented on Homer's framing story for Demodocus's second song. It seems the Phaeacians' dance reminded him of a similar Spartan dance: "Leaping up to a high point before dropping down to earth, they executed many alternations with their feet. They called it 'doing the tong-dance'" (Diels-Kranz 88B36). If this is not a reductive commentary on the text of *Odyssey* (8.376) and evidence of how well he interpreted poetry, it is certainly evidence of Critias's notorious overestimation of the beauties of the Spartan regime and its culture.

shoe-makers," and the like; but once their meaning is properly understood, they are so divine that those who think him a bore are the ones who end up laughable (221e–222a). Socrates' cosmology is expressed in rustic, shamanistic imagery, but it is closer to the truth than Timaeus's physics. A reader of the *Odyssey* understands the significance of the poet's portrayal of a poet by attending to the text's composition. So, too, a reader of the *Timaeus* and *Critias* will understand the philosophic significance of Plato's presentation of Pythagorean philosophy by attending to the literary features of the dialogues. The framing story of the *Timaeus* and *Critias* leads one to consider the basis of Timaeus's account in the cosmology suggested by Demodocus's song; and from a sense of the limitations of Pythagoreanism implicit in the comparison, the significance of Socrates' dramatic silence leads further to the erotics of the *Phaedrus* and the account of philosophy in the *Republic* and the *Laws*.

In Demodocus's song, Aphrodite, the wife of Hephaestus, commits adultery with Ares. The contractual bonds of her marriage are not as strong as the erotic bond she has with her lover. When Hephaestus learns of the affair that has fouled his bed, he sets to work and prepares a trap (*dolos*, 8.276) to ensnare the two. Hephaestus, famed for his craftsmanship (*klutotechnēs*, 8.286), makes a remarkable net that is both invisible to the gods and strong enough to resist all their efforts to break its bonds. He then arranges it, like a spider's web, around the bed, and leaves on a trip. The lovers' passionate embraces utterly entangle them in the net, of course, and they cannot escape discovery. Hephaestus's cunning has forged bonds stronger than the bonds of eros between two gods; his *technē* has imitated the order of the cosmos into which the gods were born, and even seems to have mastered it. In his anger, Hephaestus calls on them all to witness the adultery: "Father Zeus (*Zeu pater*) and all you other blessed immortal gods, come here to see a ridiculous thing (*erga gelasta*)" (8.306–7). They do come— except the goddesses, who refrain from modesty. And they do laugh—except Poseidon, who is friend to the murderous Ares. However, it is not apparent what amuses them most. Is it the plight of the lovers, whose eros is weaker than

Hephaestus's craft? Is it the humiliation of Ares, the swiftest of the gods, in being bettered by the lame Hephaestus? Or is it the spectacle of Hephaestus, so bitter that he is unashamed to be known as a cuckold? Is it the cleverness of the trap? Or is it Hephaestus's presumption in attempting to master the order of things with base techniques and command Zeus's will with appeals to contractual proprieties? Zeus ignores his demands. Apollo asks Hermes, Zeus's messenger and a god also known for his inventiveness, if he would be willing to be so trapped with Aphrodite. Hermes not only wishes it, but also says he would endure three times the bindings, and the laughter of Zeus and the gods approves his preference (8.334–43). Ares and Aphrodite, in contrast, are no longer in the mood. When the bonds are released, they quickly escape in opposite directions (8.359–63). And Demodocus concludes his song by celebrating Aphrodite's great beauty, much to the joy of Odysseus and the Phaeacians (8.364–69).

In the centuries between the composition of the *Odyssey* and the writing of the *Timaeus,* there must have been many commentaries on this charming song. None survives. The only remaining traces of which we can be relatively certain are fragments of the works of Empedocles—perhaps a Pythagorean, perhaps also a friend of Parmenides (Diels-Kranz 31A7)—who wrote that love (*philotēs*) and strife (*neikos*) are the ruling forces of the cosmos. He begins his poem *On Nature* by telling a "double tale" of the endless coming together of many things into one through love and the endless division and scattering of what is one into many through strife (Diels-Kranz 31B17). The inspiration for Empedocles' cosmology is obviously taken from Demodocus's song, and most likely not directly from his reading of the *Odyssey,* but the features of the interpretive tradition in which he wrote are largely a matter of conjecture.[17]

17. Empedocles might have taken inspiration from the writings of Pherecydes of Syros, one of Pythagoras's contemporaries. Diogenes Laertius reports that Pherecydes is said to have been the first man to write on nature and the gods, and he gives the opening sentence of one of his books as: "Zas [Zeus] and Chronos always existed and Chthonie; and Chthonie got the name of Ge, since Zas gave her Ge as a present" (*Lives of the Eminent*

Plato's dialogues are our earliest comprehensive source for the writings of the pre-Socratic philosophers. The *Timaeus,* in particular, is indispensable for understanding the Pythagoreans. However, Plato presents their doctrines in the context of a critique. It is almost certain that Timaeus is wholly a character of Plato's creation: apart from his appearance in this dialogue, there is not the slightest independent confirmation of his existence of the sort that is routinely found for other pre-Socratic philosophers. The specifics of Timaeus's account are undoubtedly taken by Plato from Pythagorean treatises, and the literary form in which Plato has Timaeus present them—a refiguring of Demodocus's song—is in keeping with an interpretive tradition of which Empedocles' cosmology is an example, but the point of the exercise for Plato is to show a reader the insufficiencies of Pythagorean teachings. There is no eros in Timaeus's cosmos. The parts might all be present and accounted for, but it is not a whole; it is not unified and moved by eros; it does not live. Far from being comparable to the account Socrates gives in the palinode of the *Phaedrus,* Timaeus's cosmology is pale and sterile even in comparison with the cosmology of Empedocles' poem.[18]

In Timaeus's story, the cosmos or the "all" (*pan,* 29e) is made up of soul (*psychē*) and body (*sōma*), united "centre to centre" (36d–e). They are united by a divine "craftsman" (*dēmiourgos*), a "technician" (*tektainomenos,* 28c) copying a pattern, who succeeds in binding them together only when he hits upon the device of giving them "space" (*khōra,* 48e–49a, 52a–b). The demiurge is not the first "maker and father" (*poiētēn kai patera,* 28c), but he is confident that his technique imitates the father's adequately. The traces of Demodocus's story are unmistakable: Aphrodite and Ares become soul and body; Hephaestus is the

Philosophers 1:116, 119). Pherecydes' speculation on myth stands halfway between Homer's poetic symbolism and Empedocles' more reasoned poetry. However, Pherecydes is never explicitly mentioned in Plato's dialogues (cf. *Sophist* 242c–d).

18. A different argument concerning the continuities of Homer, Empedocles, and Plato is made by G. S. Kirk and J. E. Raven, *The Presocratic Philosophers* (Cambridge: Cambridge University Press, 1975), 360–61.

demiurge, and Zeus the father of all; and the net that Hephaestus uses to bind the lovers together is the demiurge's "space"— invisible even to the gods, invincibly strong, and an infinitely fine web of lines if it is anything. What has become of the bed or couch (*lekhos*, 8.269; *demnia*, 8.282) on which Aphrodite and Ares make love? It is not refigured in the *Timaeus*. Instead, the trope of the couch *(klinē)* appears, with great comic effect, at the end of the *Republic* (596a ff). The reasons for its absence in the *Timaeus* are clear enough. Timaeus's cosmology is a refiguring of the story of Aphrodite and Ares, but it is as if Hephaestus were telling it; and for Hephaestus, the net is far more interesting than the bed.

Demodocus's tale makes Hephaestus laughable. Timaeus's tale is the triumph of his revolt. The demiurge's *technē* masters the unifying and destructive forces of the cosmos, the son overcomes the father and compels him to do his will, and quite athwart goes all decorum. In Demodocus's telling, the order of Zeus's dominion is not, and cannot be, overturned by Hephaestus's devices. The craftsman's narrow sense of justice is mocked by the gods' laughter. In Timaeus's retelling, all things transcendent are seen from within the demiurge's worldview and redefined in its terms. Hephaestus does his best to copy his father's way of making, but the extent of his failure is easily measured by comparing his "ridiculous thing" (8.306–7) to the richly erotic world it cannot contain. In contrast, the pride that Timaeus's demiurge takes in his craft swells until he will admit nothing to surpass it. Timaeus says the demiurge is free to choose between several patterns or paradigms for his work. Though it would seem obvious that the intrinsic qualities of the patterns should determine which he should choose, the only way to distinguish between them, he claims, is by the result: if the craftsman's product is beautiful, he must have chosen the right pattern. The only true "good" is thus his skill (29a). He may say that he looks toward unchanging "being" as he works, but he acknowledges no good beyond being as his measure. In Demodocus's story, Hephaestus summons Zeus and the gods in anger to bear witness to the injustices done him and to acknowledge his right. In the *Timaeus*, this trope is refigured as the demiurge's speech to the cosmic gods in which he bombastically announces himself their "creator and father" (*egō dēmiourgos patēr,* 41a), but not without first attempting to suppress the fear his audacity does not entirely hide by ironically dismissing all other creator gods and goddesses—Ouranos and Ge, Chronos and Rhea, Zeus and Hera—as fictions (40d–41a).

Plato does not deny that Pythagorean philosophy has insight. His presentation of it, however, is intended to reveal its defining limitation. It has no erotics; or rather, its erotics is corrupt and requires purification. If it fails to recognize the presence of eros in the cosmos and in the relations of human beings to divinity, the power of its insight becomes presumptuous and it cannot avoid a descent through the intellectualism of the natural sciences toward sophistry.[19] The cosmological poetry of Empedocles, for Plato, is better philosophy. The "double tale" of strife *(neikos)* and love *(philotēs)* expresses both the relation of division *(diairesis)* and collection *(synagōgē)* necessary for the dialectical ascent toward understanding and the proper relation of the soul to the transcendent. Where the Pythagoreans fail, Empedocles accounts for the order of the whole as well as for the erotics of our relation to the things of the cosmos and the things beyond it.

Timaeus's skill is division, but not wanting to be found lame as a philosopher, he also cobbles together a technique for collection. The power that division seems to possess is understandably enticing. By taking the amorphous "all" that bounds our existence and dividing it with a pair of mutually exclusive categories, it is possible to persuade ourselves that we have reached firm ground and the clarity of reason. Something is illuminated by any such division, but the "all" is always far

19. Rémi Brague has argued that Plato composed Timaeus's speech so that its sections are arranged on the pattern of the human body from the head to the genitals ("The Body of the Speech: A New Hypothesis on the Compositional Structure of Timaeus' Monologue," in *Platonic Investigations,* ed. D. J. O'Meara [Washington, D.C.: Catholic University of America Press, 1985], 53–83). The effect of the arrangement is to show the tendency of Pythagoreanism toward the sophistic understanding that "man is the measure of all things," as it was flatly stated by Protagoras (Diels-Kranz 80B1).

more, and always escapes it. Those who persist in the project
of immobilizing reality with the technique of diaeresis are often compelled to surrender; some then reverse themselves and
claim that there is nothing but ceaseless flux and change. Short
of such equivocal resignation, however, two ways of persisting
in diaeresis are common. The first is to supplement the initial division with many secondary ones, creating an illusion of
the comprehensiveness of the method and the certainty of its
knowledge, if only from exhaustion. The second is to patch the
flaws of the initial division by admitting the need for a unifying "third term." Timaeus uses both these devices to create the
impression that he is as much a joiner as a splitter.

With his "first division" *(prōton diaireteon)*, Timaeus distinguishes being *(ousia)* from becoming *(genesis)* so that they have
nothing to do with one another. Before the failings of the
dichotomy become obvious, the first division is quickly com-
pounded with several others: the eternal is opposed to the temporal, the unchanging to the changing, the mind or reason to
opinion or belief, the mind to the senses, and the imperceptible to the perceptible (27d–28a). Each of the divisions should
be a further clarification of Timaeus's initial insight; and when
linked together, they should form an analytic net capable of
capturing the order of reality. However, instead of illuminat-
ing reality, Timaeus's method succeeds only in hypostatizing
its various aspects.[20] Furthermore, none of the divisions is necessarily equivalent to any other, as anyone with common sense
can see; however, the similarity of their form has fooled count-
less scholars into believing that they can be neatly assembled
into a doctrine, and the phantom they have conjured up by
incanting the name of "Platonism" has haunted the history of
philosophy for centuries. The rhetoric of Timaeus's presentation is partly to blame. He rushes to resolve all diaereses into
one—though still managing to leave it unclear whether the

20. For a comparable critique of the dangers of reasoning with "gross
dichotomies," see Paul Feyerabend, *Conquest of Abundance: A Tale of Abstraction versus the Richness of Being,* ed. B. Terpstra (Chicago: University
of Chicago Press, 1999), particularly the introduction to his unfinished
manuscript and the chapter "Universals As Tyrants and As Mediators."

ultimate division is between being and becoming, between soul and body, or between pattern *(paradeigma)* and copy *(eikon)* in the demiurge's making of the cosmos—and then proclaims that "space" *(khōra)* is the third term necessary to make everything work out (48e–49a, 52a–b).[21]

In the *Theaetetus,* Plato has Socrates divide the most famous of the ancient philosophers into two camps (152d–e, 180d–181b). On one side is the camp of "being," led by Parmenides; on the other, the camp of "becoming," led by Heraclitus and Protagoras. The men of the camp of being insist that "all things are one," which is a reasonable enough claim. But when they deny that anything ever becomes, they make themselves laughable. Socrates teases them by calling them "arresters *(stasiōtai)* of the whole." The men of the camp of becoming are no better. They insist that things change: again, true enough. But when they claim that all things are always in flux or are perpetually in motion, they make themselves dizzy and are eventually swept away in a stream of sophistry. So much for the "river men" *(reontas).* What then is philosophy? Certainly not Timaeus's method of occulting the problems of a false dichotomy with an empty third term. The worst place to end up, Socrates says, is in the space between the two camps, being pulled apart by their tug-of-war. Not even Empedocles' "double tale" of love and strife avoids being caught in the melee. Socrates places Empedocles alongside Heraclitus and Protagoras (152e). How then does Socrates escape? He takes flight; and flight, he says, "is to become like the god as far as possible" (176b).[22] In other words,

21. Speculation on space, the void, negation, death—the many determinations of nothing—is fraught with difficulties for some and pleasantly free of restrictions for others. Jacques Derrida, *"Khōra,"* in *On the Name,* ed. T. Dutoit (Stanford: Stanford University Press, 1995), 87–127, can be enjoyable reading, though it does little to illuminate the *Timaeus.* Derrida's essay is explained with some success in *Deconstruction in a Nutshell: A Conversation with Jacques Derrida,* ed. John D. Caputo (New York: Fordham University Press, 1997), 82–105. I have discussed the significance of the various determinations of nothing in modern understandings of "dialectics" in "Marx on Epicurus: Much Ado about Nothing," *Dionysius* 11 (1987): 111–45.

22. Compare the conventional reading of these passages by Hans-Georg Gadamer: "[W]ith the lone exception of the Eleatics, [Plato] saw

Socrates frees himself from tedious and contentious company by becoming a divine Phaeacian dancer.

Flight from Critias's company was not always without consequence. In the *Timaeus* and *Critias*, Socrates is a civil and amiable houseguest, tolerant of his host's rambling storytelling; even so, something about Socrates offends Critias. Within a few years, shortly following Sparta's defeat of Athens, Critias will attempt to silence Socrates by threatening him with prosecution if he continues to have discussions with the young. In the *Memorabilia*, Xenophon reports a conversation in which Socrates humorously dismisses this tyrannical coercion (1.2.32–38). Critias even attempts to implicate Socrates in the corruption of his regime by ordering him to participate in the arrest and execution of one of the opponents of the Thirty. Socrates walks away. According to Plato's report in the *Apology*, Socrates would have been executed for his actions if the regime had not been overthrown before it could arrest him (32c–e). Perhaps Critias never forgave Socrates the humiliation he suffered when Socrates compared his pederastic longing for the young Euthydemus with a pig's desire to rub itself against a stone (*Memorabilia* 1.2.30). Perhaps some other of Socrates' failed efforts to teach him something gave him offense. In the *Timaeus* and *Critias*, Socrates does not attempt to instruct Critias. Plato has his silence speak for him. Plato would agree with the implication of Xenophon's story that Socrates differs from Critias in the same way that Odysseus differed from the unrestrained members of the crew whom Circe succeeded in turning into pigs (*Odyssey* 10.203 ff); however, he uses another scene from the *Odyssey* to show it in the dialogues.

[his predecessors] all as a unit and christened them with a single name—the 'Heracliteans.' It is obvious that this way of conceiving the tradition is an antithetical development, that its real motive is the positive appropriation of the Eleatic thought of being through the doctrine of the ideas" (*The Beginning of Knowledge*, trans. R. Coltman [New York: Continuum, 2002], 104).

For his presentation of Timaeus's cosmology, Plato refigured Demodocus's song of Ares and Aphrodite, developing its subtle criticism of Hephaestus as the basis for his own account of the limitations of Pythagoreanism. In dealing with Critias, Plato proceeds similarly. Demodocus's songs of the ancient war between the Greeks and the Trojans are refigured for his presentation of Critias's story of the ancient war between Athens and Atlantis. The Homeric references form the context in which Plato caricatures his uncle's sophistic writings for an audience of readers all too familiar with the failings of the man and the brutality of his regime. And again, a fine aspect of the Homeric source text is developed as the basis for Plato's critique. Homer composed the scenes in which Odysseus listens to Demodocus's three songs as integral parts of a poetic whole. Though they seem unrelated at first, the songs of the Trojan War and the song of Ares and Aphrodite have a unifying theme—the relation of love, war, and deceit—and a single purpose: to cause Odysseus to wonder and reflect on his life. The manner in which Plato refigures the songs in his presentation of the relation between Timaeus's cosmology and Critias's sophistry shows that he understands this feature of Homer's text. However, Plato takes a few liberties in reworking the tropes of Demodocus's songs of the Trojan War. Demodocus was a poet, after all, and not a murderer.

Demodocus's first song recounts a violent quarrel between Achilles and Odysseus at a festival for the gods (8.73–82). Agamemnon is pleased to hear them arguing. According to the Delphic oracle, their dispute presages the end of the siege of Troy. Now, by Zeus's will, thinks Agamemnon, is the beginning of suffering and grief *(pēmatos archē)* for the Trojans and the Greeks. In all of Greek literature, there is no other account of an argument between Achilles and Odysseus at Troy. At the beginning of the *Iliad*, an argument between Achilles and Agamemnon over a woman brings great suffering for the Greeks and Trojans alike, but the end of the war seems no closer after the deaths of Patroclus and Hector than before (1.1–7). At first, Demodocus's song suggests something more conclusive: the war will end with a victory for the Greeks once Achilles and

Odysseus resolve their somewhat Machiavellian debate over the respective utilities of force and cunning. However, there can be no triumph when the suffering of the victors and the vanquished is the same. When Demodocus sings of the sufferings of the Trojans "and the Greeks," the theme that distinguishes the *Odyssey* from the *Iliad* is sounded: the education of Odysseus in the brutality and injustice of war. Odysseus covers his head and weeps, pouring libations to the gods whenever Demodocus pauses, and King Alcinous alone understands his actions (8.83–95).

Following the contests that Alcinous orders as a diversion for the lamenting Odysseus, the wonderful song accompanying the divine dancing of the Phaeacians, and the feasting and drinking during which Odysseus takes his leave of Nausicaa,[23] Odysseus—still unknown to the Phaeacians—asks Demodocus to sing of Troy again (8.474–98). He asks him to recount the story of "the building of the horse of wood" *(hippou kosmon aeison dourateou)*, the deceit *(dolon)* that Odysseus contrived to bring about the fall of Troy (8.492–94). The song of Aphrodite and Ares has deeply moved him. If Demodocus's first song raised the question of his responsibility for the suffering caused by the war and intimated the measure against which he could judge the justice and injustice of his actions, Demodocus's song of Aphrodite and Ares has brought it home to him: Odysseus asks to hear his most cunning and glorious actions at Troy described in the very words that Demodocus used to portray Hephaestus's trap *(dolos*, 8.276). Demodocus's second song of Troy tells the story of the night that Troy fell (8.499–520). The deceit of Odysseus's horse would likely have been detected had it not been Troy's fate *(aisa*, 8.511) to be defeated. However, once the sack begins, Demodocus says, Odysseus is far worse than a clever engineer. More ruthless than Achilles, Odysseus sets out "like Ares" *(ēut' Arēa)* and engages in the "most terrible fighting" *(ainotaton polemon*, 8.518–19) he had ever experienced.

23. There is no better commentary on Odysseus's leave-taking than Nietzsche's brilliant aphorism: "One should part from life as Odysseus parted from Nausicaa—blessing it rather than in love with it" *(Beyond Good and Evil*, no. 96).

In one of the most beautiful scenes in the *Odyssey*, Odysseus weeps (8.521–32). He weeps openly, without covering his head. Homer says his tears are "pitiful" (*eleeinon*, 8.531), and in a stunning simile, he compares them to the tears a woman cries in "pitiful grief" (*eleeinotatōi akhei*, 8.530) when her city falls and her husband is slaughtered before her eyes and, as he is dying, the conquering soldiers force her away with her children, making slaves of them all. Demodocus sings of Odysseus the conqueror; Odysseus weeps with the conquered women. The rebellious cleverness of Hephaestus, once unfettered, reveals itself as the ruthlessness of murderous Ares. Demodocus's song has shown him who he is and compelled him to understand. Odysseus is finally ready to return home.

At the beginning of the *Timaeus*, when he realizes that his favored companion preferred not to be Critias's guest today, Socrates is likely ready to return home right away. He stays, however, to hear out his insistent host. In composing Critias's two speeches, Plato refigures the elementary features of Demodocus's two songs of Troy. He distinguishes the singing of the songs from their content, using the events in a formal or structural sense: Critias is thus made to speak before and after Timaeus. And the circumstances of the episode described in the first song are also deliberately echoed in the drama of the dialogues: Odysseus's dispute with Achilles at a religious festival shortly before the fall of Troy becomes Socrates' encounter with Critias during the celebration of the Plynteria shortly before the fall of Athens.

The differences between Socrates and Critias are muted by their courtesies, but they are nonetheless evident. They do not erupt in a heated argument to rival the violent quarrel between Odysseus and Achilles, heard throughout the Greek camp, because they have discussed their disagreements before, and the polarity of their opposition is already well known in Athens, if only in rumors. The circumstances allow Plato to distinguish radically between two aspects of Homer's poetic symbolism: the cunning Odysseus who becomes more brutal than Achilles is distinguished from the Odysseus who listens to Demodocus and is transformed; and the Demodocus who sings well of conquest is distinguished from the Demodocus who is able to teach Odysseus. Because Socrates already understands what Demodocus shows Odysseus about himself, and because Critias never will, though he fancies himself a poet and a philosopher, Plato makes Critias's speeches the locus of the worst aspects of Homer's portrayal of Demodocus's art and Odysseus's character. The rest is stated by Plato in Socrates' silence.

The devices of Hephaestus are central to Plato's presentation of Timaeus's cosmology; so, too, the "deceit" (*dolon*, 8.494) of Odysseus is the main feature of Plato's composition of Critias's elaborate tale. Critias's deceit is, in part, his sophistic technique and, in part, the substance of his remarks. In the *Symposium*, the tragedian Agathon, who had been educated by Gorgias, demonstrates his teacher's rhetorical technique with the opening sentence of his encomium: "I want first to say how I must speak, and then to speak" (194e). Plato has Critias's two speeches similarly illustrate his sophistic devices: the first is about the story he will tell; the second is the story itself. Although the *Odyssey* provides Plato with the literary context for Critias's speeches, and with some of his tale's most intriguing elements, the largest part of their substance is likely derived from the writings of Critias himself, almost all of which are lost. Critias wrote tragedies as well as treatises and orations; he even composed verse presentations of the constitutions of Athens and Sparta. Plato must have read it all. The largest surviving fragment of his works is from *Sisyphos*, one of the tragedies. It gives a revealing account of deceit.

The fragment (Diels-Kranz 80B25) presents an unmistakably sophistic description of the relation between *physis* and *nomos*, often criticized in the dialogues. Originally, human life was "unordered and bestial," it claims, with no reward for the excellent or punishment for the wicked. In such difficult circumstances, laws were established as "tyrant of all"—by the excellent, one is to assume—and those who transgressed them were punished. The tyranny of a regime's laws is thus the origin of "justice." However, Critias's text continues, even the ruthless enforcement of the laws could not prevent "crimes committed in secret." Therefore, "a wise and knowing man *(sophos gnōmēn anēr)* invented *(exeurein)* fear of the gods for mortals, that there would be a terror *(deima)* to the wicked even if they did, said, or thought anything in secret." He invented "the divine" *(to theion)*, and he described it to the many using "the most alluring of legends, covering the truth with a false tale *(pseudei kalypsas tēn alētheian logōi)*." Critias goes so far as to compose a speech that might serve as a model for a lawgiver's public presentation of his political theology. He then explains how the story comes to be persuasive and effective. Human beings generally fear storms, lightning, and thunder, he says, and they do not understand the revolutions of the heavens, the work of Chronos, the wise craftsman *(tektonos sophou)*. By making the sky or the heavens the home of omnipotent and omniscient divinities, therefore, the lawgiver will cause human beings to fear their powers. In this manner, the fragment concludes, "someone persuaded the mortals to believe *(nomizein)* in the existence of a race of gods."

It is no wonder that Timaeus is a welcome houseguest. He and Critias invent speeches about the gods with the same devices *(Timaeus* 40d–41d; *Critias* 107b). Indeed, Timaeus and Critias see eye to eye on most things. In his refiguring of Homer, Plato uses the trope of the continuity of Demodocus's three songs to illustrate their agreement. The theme of the significance for human beings of the relation between Ares and Aphrodite, implicitly stated in Demodocus's first song, is resolved for Odysseus when he recalls the second song while listening to Demodocus's third: the final song describes Odysseus's spiritual descent at Troy, but the instruction of the three together furthers his spiritual ascent. In the *Timaeus* and *Critias*, Socrates must sit still and be instructed by his host, whose first speech suggests that Socrates' account of justice yesterday was entirely wrong, and whose final speech, professing to do the whole job better, is a yarn that projects his ambitions in the current political circumstances onto a canvas of cosmic proportions, as Timaeus has stretched it out for him. Timaeus's cosmology corrects Socrates' recounting of Er's tale, and Critias understands the rest of the discussions reported in the *Republic* to be reducible to the paradigm of the *kallipolis*, a blueprint for a garrison regime that he finds an attractive idea. Critias's story of the war between Athens and Atlantis is thus his redescription of the city whose pattern is laid up "in the heavens" (*en ouranōi*, Republic 592b), as he and Timaeus understand the heavens, for Socrates' further instruction.

Critias dismisses Socrates' account as a "fable," a *mythos*, which he will translate into "truth," *alētheia*. Socrates scoffs at Critias's conceit with his usual irony (26c–e). There is no need to speak, because he knows the invention will never get off the ground. When asked, neither Timaeus nor Critias could recall anything from the *Republic* that gave evidence of a philosophical *mania*. When Socrates tested them again by suggesting that the stasis of an animal in a painting is no different than the stasis of a living animal at rest (19b), both Timaeus and Critias took him seriously.[24] How then could Timaeus's cosmology be expected to account for the erotic participation of living things in the "all" (*pan*, 29e)? It does not: his speech is an autopsy report. How then could Critias's plan to put the inert *kallipolis* in motion be anything other than a sophist's technical exercise? In large part, it is not. And where it is not tedious, it is worse. By the end of Critias's story, the self-indulgence of the intellectual has paled and the ambitions of the tyrant have begun to show through.

Critias's story is not the feat of anamnesis he claims it to be. Nor is it a tale passed down from time out of mind. Shortly after Timaeus's disquisition, Critias lets slip that he is speaking "on the spur of the moment" (*parakhrēma*, 107e). To be precise, he is making it up, improvising from notes made hastily last night. Yesterday, Socrates recited the discussions that constitute the *Republic* from memory. Critias is driven to top him. He will recall a tale, at least as long and far more significant, a tale he heard only once, and several decades ago at that, when he was a mere child of ten. It's a gift . . . and what is more, it runs in the

---

24. The convention among scholars is to take Socrates' remarks seriously as well. See Thomas K. Johansen, "Truth, Lies, and History in Plato's *Timaeus-Critias*," *Histos* (University of Durham) 2 (1998).

family: he heard it from his ninety-year-old grandfather, who had himself memorized it on one hearing, many, many decades earlier. And more: it is not idle chatter from the Piraeus, but has to do with Solon and world-historical things. Critias's intent is obvious. He will speak as a wise man, capable of inventing "the most alluring of legends, covering the truth with a false tale," in the words of the *Sisyphos* fragment. His policy will be occulted by the deceit of deriving it from Solon, and then again, by deriving Solon's policy from the sages of the Egyptian priesthood. The business might have been amusing had he pulled it off, but there are so many gaffes in his effort to concoct a pedigree for the story that Socrates' silence is the height of discretion.[25] Most of the narrative enigmas concern a text that disappears and reappears, and sometimes changes its character.

The war between Athens and Atlantis, he says, occurred nine millennia ago. The events were written up—the details are unclear—and the text found its way to an Egyptian library. While traveling in Egypt, Solon met some priests who knew of it. Before showing him the "actual writings" (24a), however, they taught him hermeneutics: ancient stories of the gods, they explained, are fables, the truth of which lies in natural phenomena (22c–d). After Solon returned to Athens, the Egyptian text in hand and the interpretive principles of Critias's clever priests clearly in mind, he set to work writing his own version of the tale with the intent of superseding Homer and reinventing Greek culture. Alas, pressing worldly affairs prevented him from finishing. Perhaps poetry is an idle pastime

25. When the dialogues are read as treatises and everything said in them is attributed directly to Plato, forced interpretations are unavoidable. The assimilation of Critias's sophistic storytelling to Plato's philosophy, in particular, has resulted in exotic claims. With a combination of hermeneutic naïveté and hypersophistication, Eric Voegelin argues that the author is present in the dialogues as characters best named "Timaeus-Plato" and "Critias-Plato." Timaeus-Plato "sing[s] the poem of the Idea," only hinted in the *Republic*, and Critias-Plato both narrates the "true story" of the embodiment or realization of the Idea in epic form and explores "the mythical forces of the collective soul" about which Socrates knew little. See his "Plato's Egyptian Myth," *Journal of Politics* 9:3 (1947): 311, 320; and *Plato and Aristotle*, vol. 3 of *Order and History* (Baton Rouge: Louisiana State University Press, 1957), 180.

after all. At this point in the genealogy, the text gets lost—or rather, Critias gets lost in his own story. He continues: Solon told his friend Dropides about the ancient tale; it does not seem that he showed him a text or recited the story verbatim. Then Dropides told his son Critias, the namesake and grandfather of Critias the tyrant—again, no text, no recitation and memorization. In attempting to establish his family lineage, our narrator muddles the textual lineage and eventually attempts to cover the blunder by saying that his grandfather "heard" the story directly from Solon (25d).

For all its intrinsic importance, and for all the effort one would imagine to be necessary to memorize and retain it, the elder Critias did nothing with the story his whole life. At the age of ninety, a passing remark precipitated his single performance of the text, at which the young Critias chanced to be present. Similarly, Critias does nothing with his knowledge of it—nothing, that is, until the opportunity arises to teach Socrates a thing or two. He recalls its every detail, he says (26c–d), yet he cannot keep straight whether he is recalling "Solon's account" (25e), or a "report of sacred writings" *(tōn hierōn grammatōn phēmē)* that accords with "the word and law of Solon" (27b), or a story told to Solon by the Egyptian priests (108d). Is he remembering Solon's spoken words or his written words, or Egyptian spoken words or Egyptian written words? And who did the translating of the original text, come to think of it? As an afterthought, but before his guests have the opportunity to ask, Critias obscures such troublesome questions, feigning clarification (113a–b). The events themselves were likely reported orally in Greek, but written down by Egyptians in their own language. Solon translated the Egyptian text into Greek. The Greek text came into the possession of the elder Critias, and from him, it passed to our narrator's possession, who learned it by heart as a child. One moment: did he not originally say the transmission was entirely oral and mnemonic? With an impatient wave of the hand and a breezy "Do not be amazed" (113b), Critias carries on.

The story of the war between Athens and Atlantis would be the most glorious ever told in Greece, displacing all other epics and histories. Critias frames his tale in such a way that it alludes to, and would seem to supersede, them all. The Trojan War is a skirmish in comparison. The wars against Persia were perhaps as heroic, but Atlantis is made out to be a far more formidable enemy. For the entertainment of his houseguest Hermocrates, the fanciful geography of Critias's tale even suggests a parallel between the ancient war and the Athenian expedition against Syracuse. The instruction of Socrates should be a relatively simple thing to work into the mix as well, Critias assumes. He does not give the matter much thought, because his poetic and intellectual aspirations, though they are great, are secondary to the political motives of his story. Beneath the fiction of ancient battle there lies the Peloponnesian War; beneath the description of the regimes of ancient Athens and Atlantis there lies Critias's ambition in the political circumstances of 407. As he lingers over the bloodier details of Atlantis, Socrates is not foremost in Critias's thoughts. He is thinking, above all, of how he and his faction will rule Athens and the Piraeus.

Critias's story is not only full of telling anachronisms and meandering digressions; it is also surprisingly dull. He begins with a cursory description of ancient Athens that says almost nothing (109b–112e). Aside from a flat assertion of his premise that its regime resembled the *kallipolis* in that its citizens and inhabitants were ruled by a "guardian" class (110c–d), the only substantive remark he makes about it—that the acropolis was dedicated to two gods, Athena and Hephaestus, both of whom are "by nature philosophical and philotechnical" (109c, 112b)—reveals more about the sophistry of Critias's rhetorical technique than it does about the regime. The rest of the account is ballast: an utterly pointless geographical description. When Critias turns to a description of Atlantis, however, he warms to his topic. It is substantially longer (113b–121c) and full of intriguing remarks. The fictional geography is merely a setting for the regime, an embodiment, as it were, of its form. The rectilinear upper plain is less important than the circular port and capital, the layout of the many canals less important than the arrangement of the regime, and the relations among the regime's ten kings most important of all. As Critias focuses the narrative, his fable slowly gives way to a type of honesty, for in the end, he shows his guests who he truly is.

It is Atlantis, not Athens, that Critias chooses to make the city whose pattern is laid up "in the heavens" (*Republic* 592b). When Socrates told Glaucon that the pattern of the just city he was seeking could be found "in the heavens," Glaucon did not fully understand his meaning, but Critias's comprehension of their discussion is laughably wide of the mark. He thinks Socrates is doubly incompetent: not only is he unable to imagine how the form of a regime analogous to the cosmic order might be made to exist "on earth," but his cosmology is impossibly muddled and mystified from the start. The description of Atlantis will show him how it ought to be done. Critias takes Timaeus's account of the rotations of the heavenly spheres as his model and sketches an outline of several concentric, alternating rings of water and earth surrounding an island on which the acropolis and the regime are located. To ornament the simple design, he adds circular walls made of different elements and metals at various distances from the center, alluding to Socrates' use of Hesiod's myth of the "metal ages" (*Works and Days* 109–201) in formulating a "well-bred lie" that the golden rulers of the *kallipolis* will tell their inferiors (*Republic* 414b–415d; cf. 527b), and more explicitly suggesting, in agreement with Timaeus's cosmology, that the planets are nothing but elemental bodies in circular motion (*Timaeus* 40a–d, 58c–59d). Critias tosses it off with the studied effortlessness of a dilettante for whom the brilliance of the idea alone makes the impression and attention to detail betrays a lack of breeding. It does not matter in the least to him that the reduction of the three-dimensional motion of the heavenly spheres to a two-dimensional pattern for the city of Atlantis shows that he understood nothing of Socrates' earlier discussion of the differences between plane geometry, solid geometry, and astronomy (*Republic* 527c–528d). His purpose is not theoretical; it is worldly and practical.

Atlantis is a fabulously exaggerated antithesis of Athens—not the ancient one, but the Athens of his own day. The port of Atlantis is perfectly circular, and the canals of its environs are perfectly rectilinear; in contrast, the upper city of Athens takes the acropolis as its center, and its port, the Piraeus, is laid out in a grid pattern, on the plan drawn up by Hippodamus, the originator of all such simplistic "division of cities" (Aristotle, *Politics* 1267b21–22). The Athenian acropolis is the city's highest point; the acropolis of Atlantis is in its port, dedicated to Poseidon, the god whom the Athenians rejected when they preferred Athena (cf. *Menexenus* 237c–d). The Piraeus is the locus of all radically democratic opposition to Athenian traditions; in contrast, the port of Atlantis, the seat of its government, houses a regime that is antithetical to democracy—a confederation of ten kings, brothers by blood (*Timaeus* 25a; *Critias* 119c). The immediate political relevance of Critias's story of the ancient war is obvious: The Athenians who defend "traditions" today, the oligarchs of the upper city, are at war with the democrats of the Piraeus who reject them. If Athens is to win the Peloponnesian War, it must be governed ruthlessly, in the manner of the Spartan regime: a military garrison defending an oligarchy in the upper city and a reign of terror in the Piraeus.[26] In telling his story, Critias suggests that he finds the regime of Atlantis "barbaric" (116d), but he does not keep up the fiction very well.

The finishing touch of Plato's caricature of his uncle is the unmistakable pleasure with which Critias describes the barbarism of Atlantis's confederacy of kings. The veil of Critias's sophistic technique slips, and he is caught longingly anticipating the rule of the Thirty. When Athens fell to Sparta, the brutal oligarchy of the Thirty was established and supported by a Spartan garrison. It governed the Piraeus through a Council of Ten, one of whom was Charmides, Critias's nephew. Critias was the most bloodthirsty of the lot. When Theramenes, another of the Thirty Tyrants, showed doubt by questioning the rate at which the regime's opponents were being rounded up and executed, Critias arranged to have him arrested and executed as well. At the end of his story, Plato shows Critias anticipating the legal niceties of executing Theramenes in his grim speculation about

26. Compare Pierre Lévêque and Pierre Vidal-Naquet, "Space and the City: From Hippodamus to Plato," in *Cleisthenes the Athenian: An Essay on the Representation of Space and Time in Greek Political Thought,* trans. D. A. Curtis (New Jersey: Humanities Press International, 1996), 81–97.

the need for a procedure—a simple majority will suffice—by which one of the ten "kings" might have another put to death (120d). In a moment of enthusiasm, just before the dialogue ends, Critias loses the thread of the narrative entirely and celebrates the great virtue of the ten (120e–121a): noble, gentle, equitable, wise, uncorrupted by their vast wealth, obedient to the ancient laws, literally descended from the god. If only the divine bloodline had not become corrupt (121a–b).

Plato cuts off Critias's story in midsentence. Perhaps this is exactly the point at which Critias had planned to end it, the conclusion of his conceit to be recalling a text Solon had left unfinished because of political troubles in Athens (*Timaeus* 21c). If so, Critias's performance as a rhapsode is no better than his accomplishment as a metaphysician. He was to tell Socrates and the others of a war between Athens and Atlantis, but his outline of the static forms of their regimes does not put either of them into "motion," as he had promised (19b ff). Athens and Atlantis remain perpetually immobile until Critias submerges them both in a cataclysmic flood. The stasis of the regimes gives way to the flux and flow of the ocean. And thus the battle between being and becoming is no closer to a resolution for Critias's efforts. To escape being caught in the melee, the only recourse open to Socrates—the only recourse open to any reasonable person—is taking flight (*Theaetetus* 176b).

Critias's speech ends as abruptly as Demodocus's final song. When Odysseus hears Demodocus describe how the cunning deceit of the wooden horse led to the sack of Troy, during which he was as brutal as the murderous Ares, Odysseus "melts" (8.522), weeping openly. Alcinous understands his pitiful tears and stops the poet's singing. The "better way," he tells the Phaeacians, is not to continue. It is time to send the stranger home. But first Alcinous asks him who he is (8.543–52). Now that Demodocus's songs have revealed him to himself, and now that he is certain that he is among people who will recognize him, he tells them his name: "I am Odysseus, son of

Laertes" (9.19). The Phaeacians graciously offer to transport him on one of their magical ships—ships that understand "the thoughts and minds of men, and know the cities and rich fields of all peoples" (8.559–60; cf. 1.3)—though it will bring them great troubles. Poseidon is already angered because the Phaeacians freely transport everyone. When the god learns that they have assisted Odysseus in his homecoming, he is likely to cover their island with a mountain and drown the Phaeacians in his rage (8.564–71), just as his son, Polyphemos the Cyclops, had attempted to destroy Odysseus's ship, hurling huge boulders at it (9.481–86, 537–42).

In Plato's refiguring of the song, it is Critias who becomes as brutal as the murderous Ares. The longer he speaks, the less his sophistic cleverness conceals the intent of his words; and with his praise of the ten, he finally identifies himself. He need not say any more. Even if he would continue speaking, the homecoming of Alcibiades silences him. There has been enough talk. Why spin out the false tale when Alcibiades' return makes it possible to uncover its truth? What of Socrates' homecoming? He stands before Critias and his guests, the transformed Odysseus, but he is not recognized. The omens are unfavorable when Alcibiades sails into the Piraeus during the celebration of the Plynteria. Athena is veiled. Athens has gone down to the Piraeus. Soon it will fall. Socrates' homecoming, if it is not to be today, must wait until he is with his true companions. And yet it will come. In Critias's house, Socrates is no one, but Critias can do as little as the Cyclops to stop him.

Ascent

The *Phaedrus*

The *Timaeus* and *Critias* are traditionally considered separate dialogues, and the *Critias* incomplete. The question of their dramatic and substantive unity thus almost never arises. The *Phaedrus* has always been thought a finished and self-sufficient dialogue, but it has nonetheless been found awkward and troublesome by scholars. There is little agreement about the dialogue's "thematic unity." It seems cumbersome, always on the verge of breaking apart into two halves: the discussion of erotics with which it begins and the discussion of rhetoric with which it concludes. Some scholars have been satisfied to dismiss its arrangement as "Gothic," citing it as evidence that an elderly Plato had "lost the power of composition." Others consider its unity to be principally an "artistic" feature, but they find the divers literary styles of the dialogue an obstacle to their argument. And yet, the integrity and beauty of the dialogue's literary form are undeniable. How could a work so well written not have a "thematic unity"? In recent years the question has been re-opened, but little progress has been made toward a satisfying answer.[1]

G. J. de Vries considers the organizing motif of the *Phaedrus* to be the "persuasive use of words." This is far too impressionistic. And it might be said with equal truth of almost any Platonic dialogue. Charles Griswold, in contrast, is too forced in his argument that a theme of "self-knowledge" solves the "problem of the unity of the *Phaedrus*." Complementing his account of Platonic philosophy as a qualified form of the "self-knowledge" most fully developed in Hegelian idealism, Griswold defends a hermeneutic that stresses the "organic unity" of each dialogue to the point of rejecting as "implausible" any approach that considers the "Platonic corpus" to be the "primary whole" against which a dialogue should be understood. Giovanni Ferrari has a much better ear for Plato's poetic "mode of exposition," and an equally sensitive understanding of the problems of reflexivity associated with a philosophical probing of the nature of philosophy. And yet, Ferrari says he prefers not to "struggle too hard . . . to unify the *Phaedrus*," glossing the question of the text's disparate topics by arguing that it is Plato's intent to let "the rough edges of the world poke through the joints of his dialogue."[2] This seems more an eloquent side-stepping of the issue than a convincing explanation.

1. This summary of the range of scholarly opinion is based on the discussion in G. J. de Vries, *A Commentary on the "Phaedrus" of Plato* (Amsterdam: Hakkert, 1969), 22–24. Most works on the *Phaedrus* published since de Vries' commentary fall well within the parameters of its typology. It is worth noting that almost all of the papers presented at the 1989 Symposium Platonicum, devoted to the *Phaedrus*, are topical studies. The paper by Luc Brisson, "L'unité du *Phèdre* de Platon: Rhétorique et philosophie dans le *Phèdre*," is an exception. See Livio Rossetti, ed., *Understanding the "Phaedrus": Proceedings of the II Symposium Platonicum* (Sankt Augustin, Germany: Academia-Verlag, 1992).

2. De Vries, *Commentary on the "Phaedrus*," 23; Charles L. Griswold Jr., *Self-Knowledge in Plato's "Phaedrus"* (New Haven: Yale University Press, 1986), 2–9, 157–58, 15; G. R. F. Ferrari, *Listening to the Cicadas: A Study of*

The relation of rhetoric to erotics, for Plato, cannot be understood apart from its relation to dialectic and poetry *(poiēsis)*. In
the *Phaedrus,* Socrates says that the power *(dynamis)* of speech is
leading the soul *(psychagōgia)* by persuasion. Knowing how to
speak well necessarily requires a knowledge of the soul: its various types or classes, its underlying nature, its place in the order
of things. And knowing how to lead a soul properly requires
an understanding of the forms and ends of the human soul's
development as well as an appreciation of the various ways in
which speech leads to those ends (271c–d, 277b–c). Erotics is,
in part, the knowledge of the soul's place in, and relation to,
all that is; but it is not only knowledge. More important, it is
the practice that defines a philosopher's way of life. A philosopher might, on occasion, judge the techniques of rhetoric to
be useful, and perhaps even necessary, for persuading others.
However, for Socrates, dialectic is the way of speaking most
appropriate for engaging others. Dialectic is the conversational
form best suited to a mutual encountering of the other in joint
inquiry. Rhetoric, at its best, might lead the other—assuming
he is willing—toward such an encounter. But dialectic is also
Socrates' term for a solitary practice. In the *Symposium,* he describes the soul's ascent of the "rising steps" of the ladder of
love toward the "perfect revelations" as an activity that is ultimately done alone (209e–212a). In the *Republic,* the highest form
of erotics is the highest form of dialectic: a "journey" *(poreia)* un-
dertaken by oneself, in relation to the things themselves (532a–
c). Whenever Socrates speaks of these things, and to whomever
he speaks, he must speak as a poet. Dialectic then becomes a
"song" *(Republic* 531d), and erotic and music *mania* become indistinguishable *(Phaedrus* 248d).

In Ronna Burger's apt phrase, the unifying theme of the *Phaedrus* is "erotic dialectics."[3] I do not understand this to mean
that the dialogue is a dramatized treatise in which Plato depicts

---

Plato's "Phaedrus" (Cambridge: Cambridge University Press, 1987), 1–2,
30–32, 232.
   3. Ronna Burger, *Plato's "Phaedrus": A Defense of a Philosophic Art of Writing* (Tuscaloosa: University of Alabama Press, 1980), 6.

Socrates engaging, with passion, in the intellectual or noetic pursuit of the ideas of things themselves. Plato's Socrates is no idealist.[4] Rather, the *Phaedrus* shows that Socrates' knowledge of how to speak well, his mastery of the many ways of speaking, even dialectic, is always subordinate to the proper practice of erotics. Socrates has no illusions about Phaedrus's character. He knows that Phaedrus is caught up by the passions of pederasty and will read any trashy thing that excites them, and he understands that if he were to attempt to persuade him of the beauties of higher forms of eros, he would likely have to speak in a variety of ways—using whatever it takes to hold Phaedrus's attention for a moment—about the things that most interest him, beginning with the text he is reading when they meet. Plato does not exhibit Socrates' mastery of the theory and practice of rhetoric, dialectic, and *poiēsis* to amuse or engage those of his readers similar in character to Phaedrus. He writes the dialogue to address promising students, particularly those familiar with the techniques of Protagoras, Gorgias, Polus, and Thrasymachus; indeed, he goes so far as to make a direct appeal to Isocrates, who had founded a successful school

---

4. It is not my intention, by this remark, to defend the widely accepted distinction between the "historical" Socrates, who was not an idealist, and Plato, who ostensibly was. I mean that Plato, as well, was no idealist. One can discuss types of knowledge, the nature of intellection, even the nature of ideas themselves without being an idealist. The assumption of Plato's idealism, first argued by the ancient philosophers before being taken up by Christian theologians, who made it the cornerstone of their critique of the limitations of all philosophy, has become an unshakable conviction in received scholarly opinion. It is often evident in interpretations of dialogues that treat statements about reality as if they were identical to statements about the intellection of reality. Concerning the *Phaedrus*, for example, Griswold reduces the dialogue's account of the human soul's erotic participation in the existential order to an instance of the "self-knowledge theme" by claiming that it describes "the soul's function in a 'cosmos' or 'Whole,' a crucial element of which are the Ideas" (*Self-Knowledge in Plato's "Phaedrus,"* 3). The existing cosmos is thus reduced to the "whole," a metaphysical category that, at best, stands for the intellection of the cosmos; the "whole" is then reduced to a collection of "Ideas." In this way, the *Phaedrus*, and every other significant Platonic dialogue, is made to seem an accessibly written prolegomenon to an unwritten *Phenomenology of Mind*.

for rhetoric in Athens (279b). In reading Socrates' discussion of rhetoric, Plato would have them drawn toward the practice of dialectic and, through dialectic, away from the corrupting eros of sophistry toward the eros of a Socratic philosophic life.

An initial understanding of the thematic relation of the dialogue's two halves is necessary, but not sufficient, to answer the more perplexing question of their aesthetic relation. The end toward which the dialogue moves a reader is common to all human beings. One need not be a student of rhetoric to be able to follow Socrates' direction in attaining it. The discussion of erotics, therefore, is independent of the discussion of rhetoric, and if the latter is intended as an introduction to the former, even if only one of many possible introductions, would it not have made more sense to begin with it rather than conclude with it? This feature of the *Phaedrus* will always seem an awkward construction if we read the dialogue as a text whose "organic unity"—to use Griswold's terms—is independent of the "Platonic corpus" that is its "primary whole." In other words, the *Phaedrus* is not self-sufficient; it must be read together with other dialogues if its composition and meaning are to be understood. The *Phaedrus,* in particular, must be read as the work of a poet, and one that refers beyond itself to other episodes of his epic project.

Furthermore, the literary form of the *Phaedrus* will not be adequately appreciated if it is read strictly as a "dialogue." A conversation between Socrates and an interlocutor, expressing the gradually changing character of their relations with one another, perhaps showing some development toward a better understanding of their topic, often carries much of the weight of Plato's meaning. And sometimes it does not. None of Socrates' interlocutors is ever shown grasping the full significance of his remarks, but Plato writes in such a way that their meaning will always be evident to a careful reader. Some of Socrates' interlocutors are better conversationalists than others, some are more dialectical in nature, some are more open to his persuasion, and they have widely differing characters and levels of intelligence. When Plato has Socrates engage in a lengthy discussion with someone who is unlikely to learn anything or be benefited in any way by it, a reader should not expect to find Plato's meaning in their conversation. It is more likely to be found in his artful writing.

The opening scene of the *Phaedrus*, for all that it is beautifully evocative, does not hold much promise for an interesting conversation. Plato begins the action with a chance encounter between Socrates and Phaedrus, who has been studying a text by Lysias. He intends the reader to recall both the *Republic* and the *Symposium*. Lysias, one of Cephalus's sons, was present during the discussions reported in the *Republic*. His silence throughout shows him to be either unable to understand Socrates or unwilling to participate in a conversation in which his convictions might come under reflective scrutiny. Phaedrus, in contrast, spoke quite revealingly during the festivities recounted in the *Symposium*. His eulogy claimed that Eros is most beautiful in the tyrannical power of a nonloving pederastic beloved. Neither of them learns anything from Socrates. In fact, Phaedrus paid so little attention to Socrates' account of erotics that he cannot recall the first thing about it: in the *Phaedrus*, he is still of the opinion that Eros is a god, not a *daimōn* (242d–e; cf. *Symposium* 202d–e). Lysias, who was not present at the symposium, has evidently learned of the night's events, and has paid careful attention only to Phaedrus's speech. Before the action of the *Phaedrus* begins, Lysias writes a speech just as clever as the one Phaedrus gave, which he has reason to believe will appeal to him. His text describes how the tyrannical power of a nonloving pederastic beloved can be exercised by a pederastic lover. Phaedrus, a pederastic beloved now getting on in age, is intrigued. On the morning he meets Socrates, he can think of nothing better to do than memorize it. The odds that Socrates will be able to teach Phaedrus anything during their stroll are not encouraging.[5]

5. It is common for scholars to think of Phaedrus as a promising student, open to Socrates' instruction. I cannot imagine why. I see no real evidence of it in the dialogue. R. Hackforth, for example, claims: "Phaedrus's last words, in their moving simplicity, show us . . . that the devotee of clever but hollow oratory has become one in heart and mind with the lover of truth, the genuine ψυχαγωγός." (*Plato's "Phaedrus"* [1952; reprint,

When Odysseus sets sail from Troy to return to Ithaca, he commands many ships, fully manned and loaded with the spoils of war. When he comes ashore on the island of the Phaeacians, he is alone, naked, almost completely exhausted. All his ships have been destroyed, all his companions are dead, everything is lost. A reader's first impression might be that his journey is simply a series of misadventures, but Homer's telling of the story is far more suggestive. It symbolizes the development of Odysseus's character and understanding. Of the various tropes Homer uses to mark the stations of Odysseus's spiritual and intellectual ascent, the most important concern the fates of his companions. Polyphemos the Cyclops eats his men in pairs; Circe transforms some of them into swine; the Sirens would have led them all to their death, had it not been for Circe's warning; more men are devoured by Skylla when Odysseus steers to avoid Charybdis; others foolishly eat the sacred cattle of Helios and lose their homecoming when they are killed by Zeus's lightning bolt. At each point, there is something to be overcome, something to be learned. At each point, a failure or an error leads to death. Only Odysseus survives. And when he remains alone, Homer continues the symbolization of his development with subtler poetic tropes: the tools he receives from Calypso to build a raft, fresh clothing, bathing and purification, and, eventually, the erotics of his encounter with Nausicaa.

Each of Odysseus's crewmen reaches a limitation he cannot overcome. Each of Socrates' interlocutors does as well. In the dialogues, Plato often ranks types of souls as they fall by the wayside along the path of an ascent that only the true philosopher completes (cf. *Phaedrus* 248d–e). The details of the rankings differ slightly from dialogue to dialogue, but they invariably range from tyrants and sophists to the philosopher, and have direct relevance as a measure against which Socrates' interlocutors can be judged. In refiguring the tropes of

Cambridge: Cambridge University Press, 1972], 169). Compare Griswold, *Self-Knowledge in Plato's "Phaedrus,"* 18–25; and Martha Nussbaum, *The Fragility of Goodness: Luck and Ethics in Greek Tragedy and Philosophy* (Cambridge: Cambridge University Press, 1987), 232.

the *Odyssey* across the dialogues, Plato is often quite deliberate in suggesting parallels between the circumstances in which
Socrates encounters different sorts of people and episodes in
which Odysseus loses his companions. Judging character is
not simply applying a typology, though. It is more an assessment of potential for development than an appraisal of class
and standing. One must see movement in the soul, not stasis.
Odysseus struggled to lead all of his companions through their
trials; and Plato always has Socrates struggle to guide his interlocutors toward the philosophic life. Plato would have us
see him encountering all of his interlocutors as fellow human
beings, even as we learn from the literary features of his texts
just how much or how little we might expect of them. Socrates
is particularly generous to students—those of the young in-
terested in intellectual matters, and thus prone to make the
worst mistakes. Timaeus, for example: an intellectual whose
errors in appropriating Pythagorean cosmological teachings
have led him into Critias's Cyclopean maw, but still someone
with an even chance of being benefited by following Socrates'
persuasion.

Nevertheless, the marked differences among Socrates' interlocutors cannot be denied, and some of the people with whom
he must speak are not his companions at all. Phaedrus, however, is another matter entirely. In an inspired bit of literary
playfulness, Plato bases the scene of Socrates' meeting with
Phaedrus, one of the most hopeless of his interlocutors, on
the book of the *Odyssey* relating Odysseus's encounter with
Nausicaa, the godlike woman who is his salvation. The effect
is undoubtedly intended to be comic. Moreover, Phaedrus is
made an ironic figure. In the *Symposium*, the beautiful Phaedrus, whose looks are the cause of the symposiasts' eulogies for
Eros, and the popular Agathon, whose tragedy won first prize
and occasioned the night's celebrations, are—for the moment—
the Athenians' best beloveds. The people are right to love the
best of the beautiful and the good, Plato has Socrates argue, but
they have mistaken appearances for reality and have misplaced
their love: the physical beauty and empty words of Phaedrus
and Agathon are at the furthest remove from the beautiful itself

and the good itself. In the *Phaedrus,* Plato has Phaedrus continue the role. The divine Nausicaa is present in the dialogue,
but the man playing her part has none of her character and substance; he goes through the motions, walking through the role
as her phantom. By casting Phaedrus in this way, Plato allows
himself a free hand.[6] The conversation between Socrates and
Phaedrus carries almost none of the dialogue's meaning. Plato
artfully refigures the Homeric tropes to have Socrates complete
his spiritual journey and return home as if he were alone; and
the result is a work of literature that is unusually "modern"
in its sensibilities, a work in which the author's use of setting,
plot, and dialogue becomes transparent for his immediate engagement of the reader.

Despite the initial impression a reader might have of their differences, the *Phaedrus* and the *Timaeus* and *Critias* are notably
similar in their oddly composite form. The *Timaeus* and *Critias*
seem disjointed. The promising opening, establishing a link
to the *Republic,* is followed by a series of speeches on various
topics—Critias's anamnetic exercises, Timaeus's cosmology,
and Critias's theory and practice of sophistic storytelling—that
do not become integrated with one another in the dialogic flow
of a conversation: Critias and Timaeus never engage Socrates.
The *Phaedrus,* beneath its polished literary presentation, seems
comparably disconnected. Its attractive opening suggests far
more unity than is exhibited in the sequence of topics that
are addressed—Phaedrus's memorization of Lysias's text, Socrates' cosmology in the palinode, and the concluding discussion of rhetoric. Phaedrus also does not engage Socrates as an

6. At times, Plato shows a deft comic touch. There is an amusing exchange late in the dialogue in which he has Phaedrus speculate about
Socrates' casting of people in Homeric roles. He suspects Socrates is "dis-
guising Gorgias as Nestor, or perhaps Thrasymachus or Theodorus
as Odysseus" (261b–c). Right idea; wrong names. Socrates changes the
subject.

interlocutor, though there is a pleasant give-and-take in their conversation.

Indeed, some of Socrates' remarks often appear more pertinent to the *Timaeus* and *Critias* than they do to the development of his discussion with Phaedrus. What is Socrates' ironic aperçu, exposing the reason for Pericles' association with Anaxagoras—these days, he says, the rhetorical arts "require frivolous cosmological chatter *(meteōrologias)* about nature" (*Phaedrus* 269e)[7]—if not a dismissive comment about Critias's association with Timaeus to better be able to prate about being the Solon of his time? And what of Socrates' recollected tale of Theuth and Thamos (274c–275b) that so impresses Phaedrus that he says, "O Socrates, you easily make up stories *(logous poieis)* of Egypt or any country you wish"? Do its light touch, its poetic elegance, and its brevity not make the Egyptian tale that Critias claims to have dredged from his memory a laughingstock? Even the erotic cosmology of Socrates' palinode: is it not the definitive reply to Timaeus's contemptuous rejection of the cosmology of the *Republic*'s concluding tale in his ill-advised attempt to counsel Socrates that physics is the highest philosophical inquiry?[8] Much of the *Phaedrus* reads as if it were an account of the things Socrates might have said to Critias and Timaeus had he not thought it fitting to keep a polite silence.

The structural parallels between the dialogues, as well as their stylistic and substantive differences, are the result of Plato's derivation of their literary forms from a common source

7. I have followed W. K. C. Guthrie's suggestion in translating μετεωρολογία in this context as "cosmological chatter." For his discussion of the term, see *A History of Greek Philosophy* (Cambridge: Cambridge University Press, 1986), 4:431–33.

8. There are few commentators who venture comparisons of the cosmological accounts given in the *Timaeus* and *Phaedrus,* and almost all of them prefer the scientific rigor of the *Timaeus.* Seth Benardete argues: "On the basis of the *Phaedrus* we could say that Socrates reflected on a new kind of causation, persuasion, which was unlike any known efficient causation and was not rational; and he certainly was not as speculative as Timaeus, who claimed he discerned on a cosmic scale the persuasion of necessity" (*The Rhetoric of Morality and Philosophy: Plato's "Gorgias" and "Phaedrus"* [Chicago: University of Chicago Press, 1991], 182).

text. The scenes from the *Odyssey* that Plato refigures as a basis for the *Timaeus* and *Critias* are also used as a basis for the *Phaedrus*. The *Timaeus* and *Critias* take the *Republic*'s discussion of philosophy and politics and gradually corrupt it until it seems no different than the tyrannical eros expressed in Critias's sophistic tale of Athens and Atlantis; and Plato marks the descent by refiguring tropes from the *Odyssey* that depict obstacles to Odysseus's homecoming and the lesser status of the Phaeacians in relation to the hero who must leave them behind. The *Phaedrus* takes up the *Republic*'s discussions and develops them, through "erotic dialectics," toward the political philosophy of the *Laws*; and Plato marks the ascent by refiguring the Homeric tropes expressing the Phaeacians' recognition and love of Odysseus, and the assistance they provide him for his homecoming. The tropes Plato uses for the latter dialogue overlap and subsume the tropes he uses for the former. The *Critias* ends with an allusion to Poseidon's vengeful submerging of the Phaeacians; the *Phaedrus* ends with a reference to Odysseus's final escape of Poseidon's wrath in reaching the shores of Ithaca. The ending of the *Phaedrus* fulfills the promise of its opening, which evokes the comfort and welcome the weary Odysseus receives from Nausicaa after he narrowly escapes drowning. And Nausicaa's relation to Odysseus is more representative of the true character of the Phaeacians than Laodamas's belligerent challenge to Odysseus, the tropes of which Plato refigures in the *Timaeus* and *Critias*.

The discussion of erotics in the *Phaedrus* (230e–257b) is roughly proportional to its discussion of rhetoric (257b–279b). The two parts of the dialogue are linked by an interlude in which Socrates muses about the cicadas droning in the noonday heat (258e–259d). The episode returns the reader's attention to the idyllic setting that Plato has Socrates describe in the introductory passages of the dialogue (227a–230e), and it anticipates the prayer Socrates makes to the gods of the region to conclude the dialogue (279b–c). Plato's recurring references to the features of the countryside in which Socrates and Phaedrus converse are thought by many commentators to be an attractive but ultimately unsuccessful attempt to provide a unifying literary form for the dialogue's disparate topics. However, attention to the Homeric sources Plato uses in composing the work will show that the river, the trees, and the cicadas are more than elements of a picturesque background for Plato's thoughts. The dialogue's setting is one of Plato's most convincing poetic achievements, and the most immediate symbol of the dialogue's thematic integrity.

There are different levels of generality and significance in Plato's refiguring of the *Odyssey* that make it possible to analyze the literary structure and composition of the *Phaedrus* in something of an archaeological manner.[9] Plato begins with the extensive sequence of tropes in book 6 of the *Odyssey* describing the encounter of Odysseus and Nausicaa, using it for the main features of the dialogue: the setting and its significance; the relation of Socrates and Phaedrus; Phaedrus's prior relation to Lysias and Lysias's text; both of Socrates' speeches, including the need for, and content of, the palinode; and Socrates' concluding prayer. Plato then builds on this basic structure by supplementing it with several other sequences of tropes from episodes in the *Odyssey* that he understands to be related to the scene in book 6 through Homer's use of recurring symbols and patterns of images. First, because the erotics of Phaedrus's relation to Lysias differs radically from Socrates' erotics, which has affinities with Odysseus's relation to Nausicaa, Plato reworks the Homeric scene slightly to make a purified eros the end to which Phaedrus is shown he must aspire, indicating the difference between Socrates and Phaedrus by incorporating the trope of Odysseus's relation to Demodocus in the

9. Griswold claims that in no Platonic dialogue are we "presented with a theory of interpretation (analogous, say, to a structuralist theory) that informs us how to interpret mythic symbolism" (*Self-Knowledge in Plato's "Phaedrus,"* 142). Perhaps it would be better to say that Plato informs us in every dialogue, but never presents it to us on a platter. I would agree with the first sentence of Jacques Derrida's interpretation of the *Phaedrus:* "A text is not a text unless it hides from the first comer, from the first glance, the laws of its composition, and the rules of its game." The first sentence, but no further. He grants himself complete license when he continues: "A text remains, moreover, forever imperceptible" ("Plato's Pharmacy," 63). My "archaeological" analysis of the *Phaedrus* is an attempt to uncover some of the structural laws and rules of Plato's game.

rewrite: Socrates strikingly covers his head in shame when he imitates Lysias's text, but it is uncovered when he gives his palinode. Then, rhetoric is addressed. The discussion of eros in the *Phaedrus* is largely composed of refigured Homeric tropes. The discussion of rhetoric is concerned with more fashionable, contemporary topics—the sophistic techniques of Gorgias and Thrasymachus, for instance—that are less amenable to being restated, in their details, through imagery and symbol; nonetheless, Plato sets the discussion in a frame of Homeric images. The scene of Odysseus's departure from Calypso's island in book 5 of the *Odyssey*, supplemented by several related passages from the *Iliad* and *Odyssey*, is refigured for the account of dialectic that Socrates uses as the measure of rhetorical technique. Finally, the section on rhetoric is brought together with the section on eros by the interlude of Socrates' description of the cicadas, which Plato bases on the tale of Odysseus's encounter with the Sirens in book 12 of the *Odyssey*.

The techniques of rhetoric are subordinate to the proper practice of dialectic; however, the techniques of dialectic are, for Plato, subordinate to the proper practice of erotics, and the highest experiences of erotic ascent may be expressed as readily in poetic symbol as in conversational prose. To demonstrate the primacy of *poiēsis*, Plato uses the techniques of dialectic—division *(diairesis)* and collection *(synagōgē)*—in an extraordinary way in his composition of the *Phaedrus*. Eros brings together, and rhetoric, at best, analyzes or distinguishes: collection and division. Plato bases the section of the *Phaedrus* in which erotics is discussed on the scene of Odysseus's encounter with Nausicaa. However, in his refiguring of Homer's tropes, he divides one of the most important of them in two: Odysseus's first words to Nausicaa, spoken from a divided heart, become Socrates' two speeches about eros. Then Plato delimits the section of the *Phaedrus* in which rhetoric is discussed by refiguring aspects of the scene of Odysseus's departure from Calypso's island. However, in doing so, he combines them with elements of several other distinct episodes to produce a single trope: Socrates' description of the true dialectician (266b–c). When erotic "collection" is the focus of the dialogue, Plato divides compact Homeric tropes to make the topic clearer; when it is rhetorical "division," Plato collects tropes that Homer has already differentiated to make the topic clearer. The techniques of dialectic are entirely at the service of *poiēsis* in Plato's masterful exercise of his art. And neither collection nor division is present in his composition of Socrates' description of the cicadas, used to relate the discussions of erotics and rhetoric. Plato refigures Homer's poetry directly into poetry of his own, just for the sake of writing beautifully.

Odysseus, exhausted, is deeply asleep when Nausicaa and her handmaidens arrive at the riverside by the seashore to do some washing; the embers of his life are preserved in a pile of leaves, the only covering he could find. Nausicaa has brought her brothers' good clothes to be washed because of a dream foretelling marriage that Athena, in disguise, has given her. The play of the handmaidens wakes Odysseus, and when he emerges from the thicket—weary, encrusted with sea salt, his nakedness barely concealed by a branch—all of them flee, understandably terrified: all except the courageous Nausicaa. Odysseus addresses her as a supplicant in a carefully worded speech, expressing both his astute awareness of the difficult circumstances and his wonder at finding himself before her, and Nausicaa graciously grants him all that he needs: he is bathed, anointed and clothed, given food and drink, and promised Phaeacian assistance for his homecoming. Despite Nausicaa's strong admiration of, and attraction to, the stranger, whose appearance fulfills her prophetic dream, she gives Odysseus good advice about how he should approach Alcinous and Arete to ensure a favorable reception and the fulfillment of her promise of assistance. As Nausicaa returns to the palace, driving her mule cart, Odysseus follows her on foot at a discrete distance. Before reaching the city, Odysseus stops at a grove sacred to Athena and prays to the goddess.

The form and details of the episode are rather conspicuous in Plato's composition of the *Phaedrus*. Odysseus and Nausicaa meet one another outside the Phaeacians' city in a setting the omphallic significance of which is a trope in Homer's story of Odysseus's shamanistic journey: initially, beside the river on which Zeus allowed Odysseus to reach land after his raft had been destroyed by Poseidon's great waves, and then moving to the sacred grove. Similarly, Socrates and Phaedrus meet one another outside the city and walk along the river Ilissus; and much of the charm of Plato's description of the setting derives from its literary origins in the loveliness of the Phaeacian shore and countryside. Nausicaa makes her trip to the river after she has a dream in which Athena, in the disguise of one of her girlfriends, instructs her about what to do to prepare for marriage; Nausicaa repeats some of the dream to her father the same morning. Similarly, Phaedrus makes a trip to the river after receiving a text written by Lysias, a friend with disguised erotic intentions; he is rehearsing the text, reciting it to himself, when he runs into Socrates. When Odysseus first speaks to Nausicaa, his words have two senses: the awkward situation requires them to be cunning and flattering, though tactful, but they are also a truthful expression of the awe and reverence he experiences in Nausicaa's presence. In the *Phaedrus*, Odysseus's speech from a divided heart is differentiated into two separate speeches by Socrates: in his first speech, he imitates the cunning of Lysias's text; in his second, he states the wonder of eros truthfully, or as truthfully as is possible for a human being. In speaking to Nausicaa, Odysseus blames the gods for causing his sufferings. The blasphemy is set right in two ways: Nausicaa corrects him explicitly, and Odysseus is purified by being washed in the river, anointed, dressed in new clothes, and transformed in his appearance by Athena. Similarly, Socrates' first speech is nothing but a blasphemy, and he too must be purified. He hears a voice telling him to recant as he walks in the river. And he recants explicitly in the palinode, in which he discusses spiritual mysteries—including reincarnation—and prays to Eros in atonement. Once he is purified, Odysseus walks to the grove sacred to Athena, where he prays that he might come among the Phaeacians as one loved and pitied. The *Phaedrus* concludes with Socrates' prayer to

Pan, before returning home, for a harmony of the inward and outward things.

The tropes of the basic structure are clearly evident: the dialogue's setting; Phaedrus's discussion and reading of Lysias's text, corresponding to Nausicaa carrying out her dream; Socrates' imitation of Lysias's text, corresponding to one sense of Odysseus's speech; blasphemy and purification; Socrates' recantation in the palinode, corresponding to the other sense of Odysseus's speech; and a concluding prayer. Plato also makes several crucial changes in the rewrite, but they are consistent with his understanding of Homer's text and are a consequence of his purpose to restate this understanding in the literary form of a Socratic dialogue.

The symbolism of the *Odyssey* is compact and overdetermined. Its shamanistic and omphallic imagery is often indistinguishable from its sexual and phallic imagery; its cosmological symbols are indistinguishable from its geographical descriptions; and the symmetry of the different senses never seems to falter. Plato separates the strands of Homer's imagery and weaves them into a new, more subtle pattern. The most obvious of his changes is his use of two separate speeches by Socrates to refigure the trope of the speech in which Odysseus addresses Nausicaa. The change would be significant if only because it indicates Plato's reading of the passage as having two senses. However, it also facilitates Plato's reworking of Homer's imagery by enabling him to use the palinode as the locus of almost all the cosmological and omphallic symbolism associated with the episode. Socrates' encounter with Phaedrus becomes more prosaic and natural as a result. The setting for their discussions retains some of its original symbolic significance, but Phaedrus is no match for Nausicaa. Plato's casting of Phaedrus, against type, leads to a further structural change: the trope of Nausicaa's dream and its enactment appears slightly out of narrative sequence, preceding the encounter in the *Odyssey*, but following it in the *Phaedrus*. This is primarily a formal rearrangement, made possible by the development of the palinode, but it also serves to indicate the erotic differences between Nausicaa and Phaedrus. Many of the literary symbols of Nausicaa's transcendent nature—her relation to Athena, if only in a dream; her resemblance to Artemis; her trip to the river and back in a mule cart; her play with a ball beside the river; and her importance as the daughter of the Phaeacian king—are refigured in the palinode, and not in conjunction with Phaedrus's role in the dialogue.

The introductory passages of the *Phaedrus* (227a–230e) might best be described as an overture for the dialogue. In modern orchestral overtures, the main themes of a composition are stated briefly at the outset. Similarly, Plato states the dialogue's main sequence of tropes once, even before Phaedrus begins to read Lysias's text. After encountering Phaedrus on his way to the river, Socrates shows he is well aware of Phaedrus's coyness (228a–c), as Odysseus had understood the hesitancy and courage of Nausicaa's manner in their encounter. Socrates asks to see the text Phaedrus has hidden under his cloak (228d–e), as Odysseus's words had brought out the hidden thoughts of Nausicaa's dream.[10] Phaedrus mentions that the river along which they are walking seems a good place for girls to play (229a–b), recalling the play of Nausicaa and her attendants. Phaedrus also wonders whether it is true that Boreas's rape of Oreithyia occurred here, and Socrates assures him it did not (229b–d), as Nausicaa and her handmaidens had likely wondered whether the naked Odysseus intended to rape them, and were reassured by his speech. Phaedrus suggests that they go farther along the river toward a plane tree for their discussion, as Nausicaa had instructed Odysseus to follow her to the grove sacred to Athena. And when they arrive at the spot, Socrates says Phaedrus has made him into a hungry animal following a dangling carrot or a bit of greenery (230d), as Odysseus had been transformed from someone resembling a lion stalking its

10. Socrates' request to see what Phaedrus is holding under the cloak is obviously intended to be sexually suggestive (cf. *Charmides* 155d), but with broad comic intent. Plato's image is partly based on Homer's depiction of Odysseus attempting to cover his genitals with a branch. But Phaedrus holds a scroll in his hand. One wonders why this passage has not been discussed at length in a sophisticated deconstructive account of the relation of logocentrism and phallocentrism in Platonic metaphysics.

prey into a man who would follow Nausicaa's mule cart tamely to the grove.

Socrates' brief remarks on the tale of Boreas's abduction and rape of Oreithyia (229b–230a) are frequently the subject of scholarly commentary, as is his later account of the Egyptian tale of Theuth and Thamos (274c–275b). The story is thought to give some insight into Plato's understanding of ancient myths, and, as a consequence, it has become part of the scholarly repertoire of hermeneutical techniques for analyzing the imagery of the dialogues themselves. Socrates mentions that it is fashionable to believe that the tale recounts an incident in which Boreas, the north wind, blew Oreithyia over a precipice of rocks to her death; and he adds that he has no time to go through all the ancient myths, providing likely rationalistic explanations for them, not only because they are too numerous, but also because he is too busy following the advice of the Delphic oracle, "Know thyself" (gnōthi sauton). When Socrates' comments are read as "irony," in sophomoric mode, it takes little effort to conclude that Socrates—despite denying it—is quite willing to "play the sophist" (sophizomenos, 229c), and that we should do the same in the enterprise of separating the rational content from the literary form of Plato's dialogues. Plato does have Socrates make unattractively plain statements from time to time, and even the occasional bad joke, but he never has him do so without good reason. In this passage, the sarcasm with which Socrates flatly dismisses Phaedrus's desire for sophistic rationalizations should not be taken as evidence of his barely concealed sophistic cleverness. Nor is it Plato's invitation to rationalize the imagery of the *Phaedrus*. If anything, the opposite. Plato skillfully weaves the imagery of the old tale in and out of his refiguring of the *Odyssey*'s imagery and invites the reader to appreciate the pattern.

Boreas is immortal and Oreithyia mortal. Boreas's abduction thus removes Oreithyia from the mortal realm, as well as from the household of her father, Erechtheus, king of Athens. This aspect of the story, with the sexes reversed, parallels Odysseus's plight on Calypso's island, unable to return to the mortal realm, and to his household and kingdom in particular. After her abduction, Oreithyia becomes the mother of Calais and Zetes, winged men who combine their parents' features in an unusual way. The union of an immortal and a mortal, for all its apparent desirability, can produce unexpected results if it is a forced combination of antithetical natures. In the *Odyssey*, with the assistance of Zeus, Odysseus resists the temptation of the false immortality offered by Calypso—as he had resisted the false immortality offered by the Sirens—and thus escapes the fate of Tithonos. Tithonos was the mortal who aspired to immortality with Eos, but lacked eternal youth and thus withered away until he became a cicada, little better than one of the human skins that litter the shore of the Sirens' island. When Socrates replies to Phaedrus's question of whether the story of Boreas and Oreithyia is true, he claims not to be clever enough to explain the meaning of mythical creatures such as winged Pegasuses. However, in the palinode, he does a good job of it. Using the imagery of the ancient myths, Socrates describes eros in human beings as the regrowing of the soul's wings. His account not only serves as an explanation for a great host of mythical creatures, including the winged sons of Boreas and Oreithyia, but also shows how the symbols of the ancient myths, which tend to dichotomize the mortal and immortal realms, are not necessarily incompatible with an understanding of the daimonic nature of eros. When Socrates makes up stories of his own, he reveals the truth of the old stories even as he surpasses their limitations. And he does it as effortlessly and gracefully as Odysseus, whose seemingly prosaic account of his travels surpassed Demodocus's songs without giving the Phaeacian poet any offense.

Plato's project of refiguring the *Odyssey* to present Socrates as the new Odysseus is nowhere better illuminated than in the enchanting scene that concludes the introductory passages of the *Phaedrus*.[11] After mentioning how delightful it would be to rest his head on the grass, Socrates describes himself as a stranger

11. For further discussions of the importance of the setting, see Diskin Clay, "Socrates' Prayer to Pan," in *Arktouros: Hellenic Studies Presented to Bernard M. W. Knox*, ed. G. W. Bowersock et al. (New York: de Gruyter, 1979), 345–53; Kenneth Dorter, "Imagery and Philosophy in Plato's *Phae-*

(xenos) and thanks Phaedrus for being an excellent guide in the countryside. Phaedrus finds it odd that Socrates does not travel outside the city, but Socrates excuses himself by saying he is a "lover of learning" *(philomathēs)* and the trees and open country do not teach him anything (230c–d). Following the Pythian's simple advice—"Know thyself"—might seem to preclude talking with trees. And yet, later in the dialogue, Socrates says that one might learn from trees such as the oak at the temple of Zeus at Dodona—provided it spoke the truth—without even raising the question of how a tree might be said to speak (275b–c). It depends on the tree, and what might be learned from it; and if there is a technique for such things, Socrates seems to have learned it from Odysseus.

A human being, by nature, is not an entirely self-sufficient and autonomous entity. To learn about oneself, one must learn about the ways in which one participates in orders of being that transcend one's particularity and singular existence. One also learns from other human beings, and, in their absence, from their writings. Odysseus famously traveled throughout the world, and beyond, to learn of the cities and minds of human beings *(Odyssey* 1.1–5), but Homer need not have traveled far to write the story of Odysseus's journeys. Similarly, Socrates needs only the account of Odysseus's journeys to learn what Odysseus learned, and what the poet knows. With a text of this sort, he says, Phaedrus could cart him around Attica or anywhere else (230d–e).[12] By reading the *Odyssey*, one internalizes it, or makes its narrative travels into one's own spiritual travels. All readers understand how this works, even if they cannot give an account of it. Building on this fundamental experience, Homer made Odysseus's distant wanderings represent spiritual travel along the omphallic pathway. Building on Homer, Plato has Socrates internalize these omphallic journeys in order to reveal the manner in which Socrates obeys the Delphic injunction to know himself. In Plato's refiguring of Homer's

drus," *Journal of the History of Philosophy* 9 (1971): 279–88; and R. E. Wycherley, "The Scene of Plato's *Phaidros," Phoenix* 17 (1963): 88–98.
  12. The scholiast recalls *Phaedrus* 230d–e at *Odyssey* 3.121.

text, Socrates' soul alone travels the omphallic route. There is no need to go abroad.

The omphalos is a constant, overarching presence in the *Phaedrus*. It is not only evoked in specific references and in the palinode's explicitly shamanistic imagery; rather, it is present throughout the text, at every moment of the dialogue's drama. The plane tree: Plato takes all the omphallic images of his Homeric source texts, combines them into one striking image, and playfully calls it the *platanos*. Socrates and the plane tree: Odysseus and the palm tree at Delos; Odysseus and Nausicaa, who is wonderfully like the palm tree (*Odyssey* 6.161–69); Odysseus and the sacred grove of poplars (6.291–96, 321–28); Odysseus and Calypso's alders, poplars, and "heaven-high" (*ouranomēkēs*) pines (5.238–40); Odysseus and the pine mast that saved him from the Sirens (2.424, 15.289); Odysseus replacing Demodocus, who sits beside the pillar; Odysseus and the olive tree near the shore of Ithaca (13.372–73).[13] All one.

Near the plane tree there is also a willow, sacred to Asclepius, who was said to have the shamanistic power to heal the sick and return the dead to life. Plato places a willow beside the plane tree in the *Phaedrus* to remind the reader of Socrates' last words in the *Phaedo* (118a).[14]

Phaedrus appreciates none of the mysteries in what he sees and hears, nor does he seem a man who has studied his Homer. He walks through his part in the drama caught up in the fantasy of pederastic lust, coy manner, and manipulative abstraction that Lysias's cheap rag intended to evoke in him. It is no wonder

13. Compare Segal, "Phaeacians and Odysseus' Return," 45, 62 n. 31, 63 n. 41.

14. In *Listening to the Cicadas*, Ferrari suggests a relation between the trees of the *Phaedrus* and the famous plane tree of Hippocrates the Asclepiad (16–17). Socrates does heal souls as Hippocrates heals bodies. More to the point, however, are the discussions of the ambiguity of *pharmakon* in Derrida, "Plato's Pharmacy," 70 ff; and Joseph Cropsey, "Plato's *Phaedrus* and Plato's Socrates," in *Political Philosophy and the Issues of Politics* (Chicago: University of Chicago Press, 1981), 238–40.

that Socrates prefers Phaedrus to read Lysias's text instead of performing it.

In the main sequence of tropes Plato takes from the *Odyssey*, Phaedrus's relation to Lysias's text corresponds to Nausicaa's relation to the dream Athena caused her to have. Lysias appears in the text he writes; under a thin disguise, he acts out his intentions in writing. Athena similarly appears in the dream she causes; however, her intentions for Nausicaa are not dishonorable, even though they are as disguised as she is. The basest pederastic eros, even if dressed in worldly splendor, is antithetical to a virgin's hopes for a marriage blessed by the gods—especially when the virgin is herself an image of other-worldly splendor for the mortal who encounters her. Phaedrus is fascinated by Lysias's account of the power of the pederastic lover; it may be greater than his own power as a nonloving pederastic beloved. In a different way, Nausicaa is associated with powerful, traditionally nonloving divinities: Athena and Artemis, the latter of whom Nausicaa is said to resemble. Indeed, Artemis is so unmoved by eros that the deaths of virgins are attributed to her arrows. Nevertheless, Artemis is a god and Nausicaa godlike in Homer's account.

When Plato refigures his source text, he distinguishes Artemis's divinity from her apparently unerotic nature. The symbols of her divinity and Nausicaa's participation in it reappear in the palinode, leaving Lysias and Phaedrus with their small, unfulfilling parts in the drama. Following form, the ardor Lysias's text instills in Phaedrus as he reads it (234d) corresponds to the courage Athena places in Nausicaa's heart; the manner in which Socrates is disconcerted in evaluating the text for Phaedrus (235c–d) corresponds to Odysseus's uncertainty in deciding how best to address Nausicaa; Phaedrus's disdainful challenge that Socrates better Lysias's text (235d) corresponds to Nausicaa's surprise at the difference between Odysseus's wild appearance and the expectations to which her dream had given rise; and Phaedrus's vow to place golden statues of Socrates and himself beside those of the nine Archons at Delphi if he succeeds in bettering it (235d–e) corresponds to the possibility that Odysseus might become a member of the Phaeacian royal family and sit with Nausicaa in the throne room amid the golden statues if he can meet her expectations. But it is all comedy and empty mimicry.[15]

Socrates' two speeches constitute the greatest part of the dialogue's main sequence of tropes. They are framed by comedy: Phaedrus's posturing precedes them, and a joke at Phaedrus's expense follows them. Because Phaedrus says nothing about golden statues after Socrates concludes the palinode, Socrates jests about Phaedrus's inability to understand the account of the processions of the immortals and mortals to the hyperouranian region by mentioning his similar inability to tell the difference between a horse and an ass (260a–d). Those who cannot distinguish horses from asses know nothing of half-asses or mules. Similarly, those who cannot distinguish between immortals and mortals know nothing of the daimonic realm between them, and Eros is the *daimōn* who interprets immortals and mortals to one another (cf. *Symposium* 202e; *Apology* 26e–28a).

Plato's refiguring of Odysseus's speech to Nausicaa as two speeches by Socrates reveals the different levels of significance in Homer's text. The encounter between Odysseus and Nausicaa is both a dramatic event that can be understood in all of its worldly sexual and psychological richness and a poetic image carrying transcendent psychic meaning.[16] The symbolic significance is not superimposed on the more natural sense, as fictions are often made to allegorize or mask narrowly human matters. The mortal and the immortal are two poles of an experiential continuum that remains unbroken no matter how well its features are distinguished and no matter what words are used to describe it. Odysseus's voyages outline an

15. Griswold has a subtle appreciation of the "bizarre comedy" of the relation between Phaedrus and Socrates (*Self-Knowledge in Plato's "Phaedrus*," 28–33, 51–52).

16. Norman Austin's *Archery at the Dark of the Moon*, 193–94, 200–202, is the most insightful discussion of the richness of the encounter.

exploration of this continuum by a fully human man, and his encounter of Nausicaa is an image of a stage in his exploration even though she is also a fully human woman. The words he first speaks to her reflect a daimonic tension between the mortal and the immortal, as well as the profane clumsiness of the circumstances in which he must speak. Odysseus is both a cunning man, always suspicious, and a man following the will of the gods reluctantly, always somehow open to the transcendent. He speaks to Nausicaa both in a calculating way and in a way that expresses his wonder truthfully. He is dangerous and threatening, naked and wild in his appearance, emerging from the thicket like an animal; but he is also a gentle and beautiful man when he washes himself in the river, as good a husband as any woman could desire. He is often blasphemous, blaming the gods for the evils he has suffered, as he does to Nausicaa; but he also purifies himself afterward. His recantations of blasphemies and spiritual follies are often left unstated by Homer, in part to show him as a hard man, but in part to allow the poetic imagery of all of his voyages and encounters to reveal the best manner of spiritual purification.

When Odysseus approaches Nausicaa, he is not sure what to make of anything. Is he among savage people without justice or hospitable people with godly minds? And what is he to make of the will of the gods that sends him into such uncertain and challenging situations? He silently considers whether he should touch Nausicaa's knees in a gesture of supplication or risk refraining from doing so because of his threatening nakedness, and he also considers whether he should praise her resemblance to Artemis in a flattering way or openly state the awe and reverence (*sebas*, 6.161; cf. 8.384) that prevents him from touching her knees. His divided heart is expressed in his words: the speech is partly supplication and partly flattery, partly wonder and partly blasphemy. The speech is itself divided into two parts by Odysseus's comparison of the experience of beholding Nausicaa and a previous experience of beholding an omphallic palm tree at Delos. The comparison comes in the middle: a mixture of praise and supplication precedes it, and a mixture of supplication and blasphemy follows it. In replying, Nausicaa grants him his desires and recognizes his virtue even though she corrects his speech about the god: Zeus grants human beings good fortune, she says, but each is good or bad as he wishes (6.187–90; cf. 1.32–34). Odysseus is then bathed, anointed, dressed, and transformed in his appearance; but he does not explicitly recant his words.

Plato refigures the speech and the events associated with it in several related ways.[17] First, the divided structure of Odysseus's speech is used as a framework for Socrates' two speeches and the interlude between them. The worst sense of Odysseus's words and deeds is made the content of the first speech; the transcendent significance of the encounter, among other related things, is made the content of the palinode. The interlude between the speeches makes no explicit mention of the omphalos comparable to Odysseus's reference to the palm: instead, Plato has Phaedrus swear by the plane tree before Socrates' first speech in order to highlight the difference between Phaedrus's explicit blasphemies and Socrates' shame (236d–237a).

Plato then uses the divided structure of Odysseus's speech as a framework for the structure of Socrates' first speech, the one in which he improves on the literary form of Lysias's text without changing its content. It is divided into two parts by a brief exchange between Socrates and Phaedrus in which Socrates claims there to be a divine presence in the surroundings; however, no explicit mention is made of the plane tree or any other omphalos (238c–d). In the final line of the speech, Socrates breaks into dactylic hexameter, the meter of epic poetry. His words—"as wolves love lambs, so do lovers love boys" (241d)—are both a perfect summary of Lysias's intent and a reference to the ominous sense of Odysseus approaching Nausicaa like a hungry lion stalking its prey (*Odyssey* 6.130–34).

The interlude following Socrates' first speech then continues the main sequence of Homeric tropes. Socrates immediately expresses a need for atonement, corresponding to Odysseus's purification: his *daimonion* has spoken and told him to atone,

---

17. Compare A. Lebeck, "The Central Myth of Plato's *Phaedrus*," *Greek, Roman, and Byzantine Studies* 13 (1972): 268.

he says (242b–c), as the daimonic Nausicaa explicitly corrected Odysseus; he claims to be in the clutches of Phaedrus's nymphs (241e), as Odysseus was put in the hands of Nausicaa's attendants; he almost crosses the river, likely stepping into it (242a–c), as Odysseus washed in the river; he is told by Phaedrus to stay in a sheltered spot (242a), as Nausicaa told her attendants to take Odysseus to a sheltered spot by the river; and finally, after uncovering himself, he washes with "the water of sweet discourse," attended by an obedient boy (243b–e).

As he does for Socrates' first speech, Plato also uses the divided structure of Odysseus's speech as a framework for the structure of the palinode. Furthermore, the two aspects of the middle part of Odysseus's speech are refigured as the palinode's two main sections: Odysseus's account of the difficult journey with many other people to Delos where he wondered at the palm tree becomes the basis for Socrates' account of the processions of the immortals and mortals along the omphallic route to the roof of the cosmos; and Odysseus's comparable wonder at Nausicaa becomes the basis of Socrates' account of the anamnetic relation between the love of beautiful sights and the regrowing of the soul's wings in the presence of a beloved in whom the likeness of the god is seen. Socrates says the flood in the soul that causes the wings to regrow also causes the soul to forget family, friends, and all worldly concerns (251c–252a), an experience Odysseus had had with Circe and Calypso, and again with Nausicaa, successfully sublimating the encounters in order to obtain his homecoming (cf. 253a–b, 255e–256e).

The palinode in its entirety, and not only its concluding prayer to Eros, is the purifying bath with "the water of sweet discourse" that Socrates requires to atone for his first speech. However, the palinode also includes an explicit reference to the trope of Odysseus's purifying bath. When Socrates describes the gradual erosion of the unsymmetrical relation between lover and beloved, he says that, at some point, the water from the flowing stream named by Zeus pours over the lover. Part of it flows into him, and the rest, rebounding as from a smooth surface, flows into the eyes of the beloved as beauty and causes the beloved's soul to be filled with eros (255b–d). Similarly, in the *Odyssey*, when the water of the river whose flow Zeus stilled for Odysseus is poured over him, washing away the sea salt, part of it flows into him, transforming his appearance, and part of it flows into the eyes of Nausicaa as Odysseus's beauty, and she says he resembles one of the gods.

There is a gentle play between Nausicaa's dreamy expectations and Odysseus's words with her that recognizing the two senses of his speech does nothing to diminish. In the *Phaedrus*, the relation of Socrates and Phaedrus is amiable and courteous, but Pheadrus's fascination with Lysias's text reveals an erotic vulgarity and rhetorical coarseness that is far beneath even the most suggestive connotation of Odysseus's remarks. In refiguring the scene, Plato uses his differentiation of the trope of Odysseus's speech from a divided heart to mark the differences between the subtlety of his source text and the broader range of experiences discussed in the dialogue. He shows the subordination of the techniques of a corrupt rhetoric to a corrupt eros by having Socrates, in his first speech, adopt a misdirected approach to Phaedrus's problems—addressing the poor form of Lysias's text independently of its content—that both the palinode's account of the mysteries of erotic ascent and its high poetic style are required to correct. But Plato goes further. He supplements the rewrite by adding references to the scenes of Odysseus's relation to Demodocus. When Odysseus speaks to Nausicaa, he utters blasphemous words that he must recant. When Odysseus listens to Demodocus's songs, he learns that he must recant something far worse: his ungodly actions at Troy. And he also learns that the purification of his impieties requires a change of heart, not more fitting words. The tropes of Odysseus's relation to Demodocus are thus well suited to Plato's purpose of having Socrates criticize the corruptions of pederastic eros existentially for Phaedrus, and not only Lysias's style in describing them.

Socrates covers his head and calls on the Muses before his first speech (237a); his head is uncovered for the palinode, and he begins it without mention of the Muses (243b, 243e). With these two simple tropes, Plato suggests all the complexity of Odysseus's relation to Demodocus. Odysseus covers his head and weeps when Demodocus first sings of Troy; however, Odysseus's head is uncovered for Demodocus's subsequent songs, both the song of Ares and Aphrodite at which Odysseus marvels and the final song of Troy that causes Odysseus to weep openly. Demodocus is said to be inspired by the Muse the two times he sings of Odysseus at Troy; however, the song of Ares and Aphrodite, rich in the cosmological and theological implications of its symbolism, begins without invoking the Muse. In refiguring these scenes and incorporating them as aspects of Socrates' two speeches in the *Phaedrus*, Plato has Socrates play both Odysseus and Demodocus. In his first speech, imitating Lysias's text, Socrates speaks of shameful things, as did Demodocus when he recounted Odysseus's actions at Troy, and he speaks with his head covered, as Odysseus covered his head in shame to hear of such things. In his second speech, the palinode, Socrates is "uncovered," in all senses of the term. His speech is a "revelation" *(apokalypsis)*, a fully erotic cosmology comparable to Demodocus's song of Ares and Aphrodite. His speech is also comparable to Demodocus's song, understood as a revelation to Odysseus: the story of Odysseus's butchery, made possible by his cunning devices, addresses Odysseus existentially, as Socrates' account of the erotic corruption of pederasty, brought about by cunning rhetorical devices, addresses Phaedrus. Socrates is "uncovered" when he recants and tells his rather lengthy tale, as Odysseus was "uncovered" when in tears he recanted his actions, and as the purified Odysseus, after revealing who he is to the Phaeacian court, took over Demodocus's role as poet and told the better and longer tale of his cosmological journeying and daimonic encounters. In the *Odyssey*, the transformation that finally ensures Odysseus's homecoming is described through his identification with the pitiful grief of an unfortunate woman. In the *Phaedrus*, Socrates' palinode is an account of the erotics he learned from a woman, Diotima, the story of which he also told to the delightful company of pederasts assembled in the *Symposium*.

Plato refigures the *Odyssey* directly in the *Phaedrus*, but he also has Socrates mention the intermediary story of Stesichorus's blindness and recantation in the prologue to his second speech (243a–b, 244a). The poet Stesichorus lived in the sixth century and seems to have made a name for himself by composing a *Palinode* in reply to the "Homer" of tradition who was said to have defamed Helen in the *Iliad*. The story of how he was blinded by reciting Homer's blasphemies and how his sight was restored through the purification of composing the *Palinode* "is not true" since it is so obviously based on the *Odyssey*. Demodocus both is and is not "Homer." The *Odyssey*'s description of a blind poet reciting tales of Troy is a likely source of popular images of the *Iliad*'s blind author. What is more, the sense that Homeric tales of the war might be dangerously irreverent or impious is already present in the *Odyssey*'s image of Odysseus covering his head—becoming sightless, as it were—when Demodocus recites his own. Stesichorus's blindness results from his similar recitation of Trojan stories, combining the symptoms of Demodocus's and Odysseus's related "blindnesses"; he regains his sight—the veil is lifted from his eyes—through a purification that recalls the trope of Odysseus's transformation; and Stesichorus thus surpasses "Homer" as a poet just as Odysseus might be said to surpass Demodocus in the *Odyssey*. Plato has Socrates pay tribute to Stesichorus's *Palinode* before presenting his own, but the equivocal compliment does more to expose his use of the Homeric sources than to honor him as a poet.

Socrates promises he will be wiser (*sophōteros*, 243b) than previous poets in his palinode. He also claims that no poet yet has sung fittingly of the "hyperouranian region" (*hyperouranion topon*) beyond the roof of the cosmos, the realm of "really existing being" (*ousia ontōs ousa*, 247c). It would be wrong to take Socrates' remarks as an indication that there is a necessary, categorical distinction between the philosophic and poetic accounts of the final, transcendent realm, or that the palinode is intended to be read as an allegorization of a strictly rational account into poetic images.[18] Plato is certainly having Socrates claim superiority to the "Homer" of tradition, to Stesichorus, and to all the poets—and the philosophers, for that matter—whose parts in the "old quarrel" between poetry and philosophy have driven it to open hostilities. However, Socrates' palinode is a poetic account. Furthermore, Plato takes Socrates' remarks from Homer himself. In the *Odyssey*, the poet Demodocus is displaced by the storyteller Odysseus, who speaks in "prose," but the storyteller's "prose" is a trope of Homer's poetry. Demodocus's cosmology, stated in "Homeric" symbols of the relations of Olympian gods, is superseded by Odysseus's tales of his voyages, which speak more directly about human nature and the relations of human beings and divinities; however, Homer has Odysseus recount his ascent to a "hyperouranian region," beyond the ostensible limitations of a "Homeric" cosmos, in even more archaic, shamanistic symbols.

The image of the covering and uncovering of Socrates' head explicitly relates the *Phaedrus* to the *Timaeus* and *Critias*. When Socrates recounted the discussions of the *Republic* for Critias and his friends, they dismissed him as an unsophisticated man. Timaeus's lecture in cosmology and Critias's sophistic exercise in political theorizing patronized Socrates, but he endured it patiently. Plato has the reader understand the significance of Socrates' silence by basing the drama of the *Timaeus* and *Critias* on the tropes of Odysseus's relation to Demodocus. In the *Phaedrus*, Socrates uncovers himself and breaks the silence. The palinode is Socrates' reply to Timaeus. It restores the cosmology of the concluding tale of the *Republic*, the story that Timaeus had thought an entirely unscientific fable because of its extravagant descriptions of the music of the heavenly spheres, the ascents and descents of souls along the axis mundi,

18. Although Socrates' evocative imagery is easily manipulable because of its compactness, it will not readily conform to modern accounts of Plato's "theory of forms," however understood. For Plato, being (*ousia*) is neither identical to form or *idea* nor a combination of form and a material substrate. Consequently, the hyperouranian region, even though it is open to intellection (*noesis*), is not Plato's image for a realm of ideas.

encounters with fantastic divinities, and such. And as soon as the palinode is done, Socrates replies to Critias. His discussion of the worst excesses of rhetoric restores the account of dialectic he gave in the *Republic,* the understanding that Critias had thought naive and artless in comparison with sophistic techniques of using words effectively in public speeches and private entertainments. If one were to read the story of the war between Athens and Atlantis in light of Socrates' discussion of the subordination of even the best rhetoric to dialectic, and the ultimate compatibility of philosophic dialectic and poetics, Critias's Solonic legend would seem little better than a poorly done assignment in a schoolboy's workbook.

In the palinode, Socrates makes reference to the theoretical problems that troubled Timaeus's physics and metaphysics. Timaeus had difficulty holding body *(sōma)* and soul *(psychē)* together. He left it to the technical skills of the demiurge— not the divine "maker and father" *(poiētēn kai patera, Timaeus* 28e)—to bind them together with "space" *(khōra,* 48e–49a, 52a–b). Socrates unites *sōma* and *psychē* with *nous;* and the divine *nous* of the father transcends the technical knowledge of the demiurge (cf. *Philebus* 22c). Timaeus also could not reconcile being and becoming, the stasis of the whole and the flow of change. Socrates escapes the dilemma: a "beginning" *(archē)* is neither being nor becoming, and motion from an *archē* is not formless flux, just as the *archē* itself is not static (*Phaedrus* 245d). Indeed, *sōma, psychē,* and *nous* are understandable as types of motions, and all may be seen to proceed from a first *archē:* the "father," divine *nous,* whatever the god wishes to be called. The discussion of types of motion begun in the *Phaedrus* is taken up in book 10 of the *Laws.* In the palinode, Socrates is more concerned with motion toward the *archē.* In the *Theaetetus,* Socrates says that one should escape the conflict between the camps of being and becoming by taking flight, and flight "is to become like the god as far as possible" (176b). In the *Phaedrus,* Socrates explains how it is done: obviously, one must first grow feathers. Half of the palinode is an account of the often painful erotics of a soul's sprouting its feathers, ostensibly Socrates' exegesis of two verses about Eros attributed to Homer by his followers: Whom mortals call *Erōs*, the immortals call "Winged One" *(Pterōs)*, because of his necessity *(anankē)* to grow wings (252b–c). The other half of the palinode is Socrates' description of the flights of divine and human souls along the axis mundi toward the roof of the cosmos, a poetic excess about the hyperouranian region that would likely bring tears of laughter to Timaeus's eyes.

Plato's division of the palinode into two sections, reflecting the divided structure of Odysseus's speech to Nausicaa, allows him to differentiate the shamanistic, cosmological, and omphallic significance of the encounter in the source text from its narrowly sexual and psychological significance. The relation between the two sections is indicated through their shared imagery: the palinode's account of the cosmic processions makes no explicit reference to eros, but its imagery of the motion of *psychē* guided by something beyond would make little sense without the discussion of erotics that complements it. The differentiation of the two sections, however, gives Plato a great deal of poetic license, especially since his refiguring of Odysseus's erotically charged encounter with Nausicaa as a far less dramatic conversation between Socrates and Phaedrus removes the constraints of the source text to balance the cosmological and sexual aspects of the story. Plato is free to augment the symbolism of the encounter by incorporating any comparable aspect of Odysseus's shamanistic journeys in his composition of the palinode. One would assume, then, that the imagery of the "grand myth" of the processions is drawn from the whole of the *Odyssey*. However, a surprising amount of the palinode's remarkable imagery is based on nothing more than Plato's refiguring of the poetic details of the encounter between Odysseus and Nausicaa. Indeed, three of the most defining features of the grand myth can be traced to Plato's use of simple Homeric tropes: the cosmos and its rotation, the chariot and horses of the soul, and the ascent and descent of the processions.

Plato's description of the cosmos grows from a delightful Homeric image: when one of Nausicaa's attendants missed catching a ball thrown to her, it fell into the swirling river; they all cried out, somewhat like the Sirens singing, and Odysseus awoke (6.115–17). In the *Republic* (485c–d), Plato's refiguring of Homer's first description of this river indicates that he takes it to be a symbol of the eros that extends from the simplest human experiences to the relation of a mortal supplicant to Zeus himself. Eros flows through the rotating cosmic sphere just as Nausicaa's ball swirls in the river. Transforming the ball in Nausicaa's hand into the cosmic sphere is not as much a flight of fancy on Plato's part as it might seem: there is a basis in Homer. Eos, the dawn, is famously "rosy-fingered" *(rododak-tylos)*. The fingers of her hand rise up from the horizon into the morning sky. She holds the world in the palm of her hand. The gods play with the world like a ball. The ball the godlike Nausicaa throws into the river, therefore, is readily understandable as a symbol of the cosmic sphere moved by eros alone. Eros flows through, or moves all things through, *psychē;* it even moves *psychē* in play and song. In the *Republic* (617b–c), Plato describes the Sirens as singers of the music of the cosmos, accepting the Sirens' own claim to be able to sing of everything that happens throughout the world (*Odyssey* 12.191). Plato's Sirens recall the playing, dancing, and crying out of Nausicaa and her attendants as much as they do the Sirens Odysseus hears and bypasses.

Plato's comparison of the chariots and horses of immortals and mortals is based on Homer's description of Nausicaa and her mule cart. The explicit comparison of Nausicaa and Artemis brings to mind the chariot and horses with which Artemis travels the heavens. Nausicaa's mule cart is not as well equipped, but it is markedly superior to Odysseus's pedestrian and all-too-human means of transportation. Plato's imagery remains relatively close to the sense of Homer's symbolism. In one sense of Plato's image, the relation of the charioteer, the two horses and the chariot correspond to the relation of *nous, psychē,* and *sōma;* the difference in the quality of the horses possessed by immortals and mortals serves to account for the different ways in which they have or move *sōma*. In another sense of the image, the chariot falls away and different aspects of *psychē* are described. Immortals and mortals alike may be said to consist of *nous*, the charioteer, and varying psychic states comparable to two horses of differing character.

What of the wings? There seem to be no wings on Nausicaa's mules. Perhaps Plato derives the image from the traditional accounts of Pegasuses that Socrates claims to be unable to explain? Or, instead, from the apocryphal Homeric verses equating *Erōs* and *Pterōs*? There are, however, magical wings in the *Odyssey*, and Plato's use of the image in the palinode is governed by his perceptive reading of Homer. The wing symbolizes both eros and the relationship of *psychē*—even the *psychē* of Zeus—to the unnamed source of wonder in the hyperouranian region. Ultimately, for Plato, the highest eros and the proper relation of *psychē* to the transcendent are different descriptions of the same thing. Similarly, in other dialogues, that which transcends the Olympian Zeus is given several equally inadequate names—the "good beyond being" (*Republic* 509b), "divine *nous*" (*Philebus* 22c), and simply "the god" (*Laws* 716c). Divine *nous* draws the *psychē* of immortals and mortals toward it erotically. It causes wings to grow on the horses of the *psychē* of human beings, it causes the wings to raise *psychē* through the cosmos, and it causes *psychē* to aspire to raise its charioteer through the roof of the cosmos.

The palinode's image of the omphallic ascent and descent of the immortals and mortals is based on several tropes in the Homeric source text that describe travel, motion, and direction. After Nausicaa's dream, Athena ascends in leaving Scheria for her home, "unmoving" (*asphales*) Olympos; no chariot and horses are mentioned (6.41–47). Artemis's chariot and horses, in comparison, travel continuously through the heavens, ascending and descending with the regularity of a heavenly body. Nausicaa, who resembles Artemis, leaves home in her mule cart, followed by attendants. If understood geographically, the journey is a descent, but if understood symbolically, it is an ascent. When they reach the river, the mules are unyoked to graze in a meadow, and when their work and play are done they

harness the mules to return home (6.81–112). Odysseus eventually follows Nausicaa's mule cart toward the city of the Phaeacians; the journey is both geographically and symbolically an
ascent. When Nausicaa arrives home, the mules are again unyoked, and she is attended by Eurymedousa, a woman from
Apeire, "the land without bounds." Before entering the city,
Odysseus must wait—the human equivalent of grazing—in the
grove sacred to Athena near a meadow. His prayer, if answered,
will ensure his homecoming aboard one of the Phaeacians'
magical ships (6.316–31, 7.1–13). In the instructions Odysseus
receives from Nausicaa before her return, he is told of the insolent and graceless Phaeacians who assemble regularly at the
harbor. They do not honor the Phaeacian ruling family; they
do not follow Nausicaa's cart to the palace, but prefer to go
down to the harbor and the sea. The boats that concern them
are simple black ships; there is no magic about them (6.262–85).

Plato's refiguring of these tropes begins with the observation
of a continuum from the human to the transcendent. Odysseus and the insolent Phaeacians represent the two aspects
of the human pole of the continuum. Nausicaa represents the
daimonic realm, and following in her train represents the as-
piration of human beings to be as godlike as possible. The
Olympian gods are immortals to which the daimons are similar. But the Olympians themselves recognize something beyond them: the unmoving, nameless pole of the continuum that
Plato discerns as the end toward which Homer's description of
Odysseus's ascent is directed. Once the omphallic continuum is
established and its various aspects distinguished, the Homeric
details of Plato's refigured account fall into place. The difference between the horses of mortals and immortals is derived
from the difference between the asses and horses necessary to
breed Nausicaa's daimonic mules. The ascent of the immortals is as effortless as Athena's ascent to her home, a home that
Plato differentiates from an "unmoving" beyond-land when he
describes the immortals' homecoming to Olympos as a descent
from the roof of the cosmos. The ascent of the mortals through
the daimonic realm has two goals: raising the charioteer's head
briefly into the hyperouranian region, just as Artemis's head is

raised above those of the nymphs in play (6.107–9); and giving
nourishment to the horses, just as Nausicaa's mules are nour-
ished in the meadow and on her return home. Those who lose
their wings in failing to attain a vision of the beyond resemble
insolent Phaeacian sailors (cf. *Phaedrus* 243c), and the wings
they lose are the magical oars the sailors refuse to take up in
order to busy themselves shaping plain oars for the black ships
in the harbor.

The ascent of shamans to the roof of the cosmos is often described as climbing an omphallic tree or sailing a ship through
the heavens. The *Odyssey* uses both images as a basis for Odysseus's journeys and homecoming: the sailing imagery is primary, but references to omphallic trees are made throughout
the poem to mark the stages of the way. The grand myth of
the processions in the *Phaedrus* transforms Homer's ships into
chariots and their oars into wings, as Homer himself does in a
passing description of Odysseus's homecoming on the Phaeacian boat that is both like a chariot and faster than a falcon
(*Odyssey* 13.81–88); and the plane tree, the *platanos*, that guides
Socrates' ascent and homecoming is beside him the whole time,
shading his journey.

After concluding the palinode, Socrates says his inspiration still
lingers, momentarily affecting his memory, and asks if he had
defined eros at the beginning of his speech. Phaedrus confirms
it, but he also responds to the whole speech by adding: "with
inexplicable excess" (*amēkhanōs ge hōs sphodra*, 263d). Socrates is
used to his "excesses" being mocked. Timaeus made Socrates
listen to a tedious lecture to prove to him that philosophy is
physics, not old wives' tales like Er's myth (*Timaeus* 29c–d).
Glaucon threw up his hands when he heard Socrates' description of the good "beyond being." He burst out: "Apollo, what
daimonic hyperbole!" Although Socrates was restrained in his
reply at the time, he allows himself an editorial comment in re-
peating the discussion to his unnamed friend: Glaucon spoke
"very laughably" (*mala geloiōs*) (*Republic* 509b–c). Socrates does

not bother to reply to Timaeus, a man who evidently does not enjoy the engagement of conversation. In contrast, he is quite happy to continue speaking with Glaucon; however, he drops the level of the discussion somewhat, to better enable Glaucon to follow. What to do with Phaedrus? Socrates is not surprised that he has not followed him very well (260b–c). However, Phaedrus enjoys conversation, especially talk about eros, even if it never seems to get very far. Despite the mockery, Socrates continues speaking with him, but he changes the topic. He had been addressing the erotic content of Lysias's text. Because this has proved too challenging for Phaedrus, he turns the discussion to a more formal, but lesser, matter: rhetoric.

In the *Republic*, when Glaucon reaches a limit to his understanding, Plato has Socrates lower the level of the discussion and try again to lead him beyond it. Plato uses the same device on a broader scale in the *Phaedrus*. The main topic changes from erotics to rhetoric, from ends to means, to lead to the end again. The discussion of rhetoric finds its place in the composition of the dialogue through its subordination to Socrates' formal and substantive definition of dialectic. And Plato, again, bases his presentation of Socrates' account of dialectic on scenes in Homer. When Socrates first discusses the formal features of dialectic—division *(diairesis)* and collection *(synagōgē)*—Plato has him paraphrase a passage from book 5 of the *Odyssey*. He will follow in the footsteps of a true dialectician, he says, as Odysseus followed in the footsteps of the goddess Calypso (*Phaedrus* 266b; *Odyssey* 5.193). As the scene continues in the *Odyssey*, Calypso leads Odysseus to a stand of trees that towers to the heavens, where he is given an ax and an auger with which to build the boat that is to take him to the Phaeacians. The ax fells the trees and splits and planes them into boards; the auger joins the boards together. In Plato's refiguring of the episode, Calypso's two tools become the two aspects of dialectic: splitting and joining, division and collection. The tools, and the boat as well, are a means to an end: they enable Odysseus to reach Scheria, where he meets Nausicaa. At this point in the *Odyssey*, Homer's narrative is in natural sequence: Odysseus uses the tools to build the boat and sets out on his voyage.

In refiguring these scenes for the *Phaedrus,* Plato reverses the order: the discussion of erotics is based on Odysseus's relation to Nausicaa, and the discussion of rhetoric and dialectic that follows is based on Odysseus's relation to Calypso. He even allows himself an in-joke about it: he has written a text whose "logographic necessity" is like "a man swimming on his back, in reverse, starting from the end instead of the beginning" (264a–b). The point of Plato's business is not to hint that Calypso pales in comparison with Nausicaa, but rather to show that Phaedrus has missed the boat, as it were, and must start over again.

Socrates begins the discussion of division and collection by asking Phaedrus if he has heard of the treatises on rhetoric said to have been written by Nestor and Odysseus at Troy (261b). There are no such works extant. Socrates is instead alluding to two speeches made in the second book of the *Iliad.* Homer's text describes the Argive troops in disarray and then relates how two speeches by Odysseus and Nestor brought them into order. Odysseus collects the troops with a speech recounting the prophetic interpretation of an omen (2.278–35); Nestor then divides the troops by tribe and clan (2.336–68). The two speeches plainly correspond in substance to the two aspects of dialectic. For Plato, division is secondary to the insight necessary for collection in dialectic, and when this insight is developed, it is possible to leave dialectic behind. In the *Iliad,* the primacy of the insight of collection is indicated by Odysseus's superiority to Nestor, and there are similar hints that Odysseus can divide as well as he can collect. It is only in the *Odyssey,* however, that Odysseus emerges as master of both skills.

Socrates' reference to following in Calypso's footsteps is part of a subtle definition of the nature of dialectic and its relation to things beyond it. Plato has Socrates say that he is a lover *(erastēs)* of divisions and collections as aids to speech and thought, that he will follow anyone who knows how things are naturally collected into one and divided into many as if he were walking in the footsteps of a god, but that only the god knows if it is right to call such a man a dialectician (266b–c). It is not only the direct reference that is taken from the *Odyssey.* Plato derives every aspect of the definition from Homer. It would seem Plato noted that the passage describing a character following in a god's footsteps occurs four times in the *Odyssey*, and that he interpreted the formal repetition to indicate a substantive relation of the scenes in which the passage appears: Socrates' definition refigures all four of the scenes at once.

In the first scene, Telemachus is preparing for his voyage in search of his father (2.406). He follows in the footsteps of Athena, who is disguised as Mentor. In the second, Telemachus lands at Pylos to inquire about his father from Nestor. Before he again follows in the disguised Athena's footsteps, she answers his question about what he should ask Nestor by advising him: Some of it you will discern *(noēseis)* with your own mind and some of it the *daimōn* will suggest (3.30). In the third, Odysseus is preparing for his voyage. He follows in Calypso's footsteps and eventually obtains his two tools (5.193). And in the fourth scene, Odysseus has landed on Scheria and learned the manner of obtaining his homecoming from Nausicaa. He inquires the way to the palace of Alcinous and Arete from a young girl, Athena in disguise, and she protects him as he follows in her footsteps (7.38). The four scenes have an obvious parallel: a son and a father are both described as setting out on a voyage, reaching an immediate destination, going to speak to the ruler of the place, and receiving advice or aid, in two parts, from a disguised or concealing divinity. But there are also several important differences. Telemachus sets out to find his father—in other words, to become like his father. It is a voyage of maturation, not of homecoming. And in order that he might find or become like Odysseus, he must initially seek out Nestor, the man whose rhetorical skills are comparable, but second to, his father's. As well, Telemachus and Odysseus receive similar, but not identical, advice or aid from their respective divinities. The distinction between the skills of division and collection is not the same as the distinction between what one discerns with one's own mind and what a *daimōn* or a god suggests. The latter distinction is superior to the former, and the suggestions of a *daimōn* or a god are superior even to one's own ability to discern how things are naturally collected in a unity. The influence of a divinity is thus beyond dialectic.

In aspiring to become like Odysseus, Telemachus must first go to Nestor, with the help of the god, and eventually he must learn how Odysseus himself follows Athena, and ultimately the will of Zeus. In refiguring Homer's rich imagery, Plato has Socrates begin by placing himself in Telemachus's position: in aspiring to become like the true dialectician, he must first learn division and collection, with the help of the god, and then he must learn how the dialectician himself follows the god.

Between the *Phaedrus*'s extensive discussions of erotics and rhetoric, Socrates pauses to express his delight in the music of the cicada choir, droning in the noonday heat (258e–259d). The interlude returns our attention to the setting, consecrated to Achelous, father of the Sirens (230b–c), and to the plane tree by the river in which the cicadas have settled. Far from being a literary distraction intended to divert the reader's attention from a structural flaw in Plato's text, as it is not uncommon for scholars to claim, the tale of the cicadas provides a graceful transition from the heights attained in the palinode to the worldly concerns that have never left Phaedrus's mind. Socrates agreeably changes the topic, and yet the topic remains the same. The symbolism of his lyric description has the same origin and ultimate end as the erotic ascent of the palinode that precedes it and dialectical ascent of the discussion that follows it. Plato bases Socrates' tale of the cicadas on Homer's description of Odysseus's encounter with the Sirens in book 12 of the *Odyssey*. Circe, the Sirens, Calypso, Nausicaa: all of them attract Odysseus, all guide him some part of the way toward the zenith of his cosmic ascent and his eventual homecoming, and all of them must be left behind. Calypso, in particular, is more than a difficult challenge and a source of tools and lumber. She assists Odysseus in his voyage to Scheria by giving him directions by the stars; in this, she resembles Circe and the Sirens.

In Plato's refiguring of the Homeric tropes, therefore, the song of the cicada choir in the plane tree, buzzing throughout the discussion of rhetoric and dialectic, is a constant reminder that the ultimate end of the discussion is erotics.

The story of the cicadas is not entirely original to Plato, as is often claimed by the more literal-minded of his readers.[19] It is so obviously a refiguring of Homer's tale—Socrates compares the cicadas to the Sirens explicitly (259a)—that it offers an excellent opportunity to observe the ease with which Plato practiced his literary and interpretive skills.

The story of Odysseus and the Sirens is in two parts: the account of what Odysseus learns from Circe before he sets sail, which Circe says the god will enable him to remember (*Odyssey* 12.36–54), and the poet's somewhat more detailed account of the events themselves (12.154–200). Circe warns Odysseus that unsuspecting men seeking their homecoming become enchanted by the Sirens' song and end up as bone heaps and shriveled skins on the shore of the Sirens' island. She then counsels him on how he and his companions might avoid this fate, but she tells him neither what the Sirens sing nor whether he should or should not listen. Once embarked, Odysseus relates the most important part of what he had been told by the goddess to his companions, including his decision to listen. Everything is made ready for the encounter. He is bound to the mast, and they remain at the oars; the ropes that bind him prevent him from acting, and the wax that seals their ears prevents them from hearing; he listens alone, and they act in concert. The song Odysseus hears is sung only for him. Every man hears their song addressing him alone: that is part of its charm (cf. Xenophon, *Memorabilia* 2.6.11–12). Odysseus is charmed neither by the pleasure of listening nor by the beauty of the melody, but rather by the knowledge promised in the song. The Sirens sing of two things: of Odysseus's words and deeds at Troy and of everything that happens throughout the world. In other words, they promise to tell Odysseus everything about

19. For example, see P. Frutiger, *Les mythes de Platon* (Paris: Librairie Félix Alcan, 1930), 233, cited by Hackforth, *Plato's "Phaedrus,"* 118.

himself and his place in all that is. This is not "self-knowledge" in the narrow sense: its full significance is made evident, if by nothing else, by the shamanistic symbol of the mast, representing the omphalos. The Sirens only sing the truth. The danger of the encounter lies within each mortal who listens, for he may forget that the self-knowledge they offer is in words alone. The separation of understanding from action is both necessary for, and a dangerous threat to, true self-knowledge. Its necessity is symbolized in the trope of the differences between Odysseus and his men during the encounter; its danger appears in the necessity that Odysseus stay on course, bound to the omphallic mast, for succumbing to the charm of words, even true words, will separate soul and body irremediably and take away his homecoming.

Little is required to transform Homer's story into the tale of the cicadas. Socrates' description of the setting is divided into two parts by Phaedrus's inept interruption. Its form thus reflects the division of Homer's narrative: the first part recounts things simply, and the second combines a more detailed description with an explanation. Plato does not have Socrates compare the cicadas and the Sirens whimsically, as an offhand remark. He refigures Socrates' account directly from Homer's imagery. The bones and skin of men on the shore of the island and the Sirens singing of transcendent things in the meadow become one image. Plato identifies the souls of the men, charmed by the song of these unusual divinities, with the divinities themselves, moved to sing of things that transcend them. Mortals charmed by the Muses leave their bodies behind like empty shells and become intermediaries between mortals and immortals. Plato uses the cicada's metamorphosis, in which its original body becomes an empty shell, as a symbol for this separation of body and soul. The cicada's metamorphosis also recalls the palinode's description of the swelling of eros in the soul as the growing of wings: all mortals may become like the gods through the intermediary of eros. Athenians are no different than anyone else, but the image of the cicadas makes the general account of the palinode particularly relevant to them. The traditional epithet of Athenians, "wear-

ing a cicada" *(tettigophoros)*, refers to their custom of wearing
jewelry in the shape of a cicada to show that they considered
themselves autochthonous, generated from the earth like these
odd insects.

Plato would prefer Athenians to become more like the cicadas than the sheep and slavish shepherds who fall asleep at
noon under their spell. The simple advice that Socrates gives
Phaedrus parallels the advice Circe gives Odysseus: better to
engage in dialogue than sleep at noonday like a beast; better
to honor Terpsichore and Erato, and perhaps even the Muses
of philosophy, Calliope and Ourania. The two aspects of the
Sirens in Homer's narrative—the danger that turns men into
corpses and the necessity of listening to them for spiritual development—are distinguished as bodily sloth and Music celebration. Plato carefully selects the four Muses he has Socrates
mention to emphasize the textual parallel. The two Muses of
philosophy, traditionally the Muses of epic poetry and astronomy, correspond to the two kinds of knowledge offered by the
Sirens. Philosophy combines them into true self-knowledge,
knowledge of oneself and one's place in all that is. Socrates
honors Calliope and Ourania; Phaedrus would do well to begin by honoring Terpsichore and Erato. Socrates honors Erato, the Muse of erotic poetry and mimic imitation, in various
ways in the dialogue. Not the least of these is his relation to
Phaedrus, which, in this context, corresponds to the relation
between Odysseus and the crewmen who would be wise to do
as they are told. Finally, Terpsichore: a chorus dances in uni-
son just as Odysseus's men row past the Sirens' island. It is
not likely, however, that Phaedrus would ever join a chorus for
Socrates.

The cicadas make Phaedrus sleepy; the beauty of their song
is lost on him. Socrates' palinode was lost on him as well. Socrates must do everything himself, it seems. Plato's refiguring
of Homer's tale thus casts Socrates in all the roles: he is partly
Odysseus speaking to his companions, partly Circe speaking
to Odysseus, and partly a Siren singing to Odysseus (cf. *Symposium* 216a). He is even the poet recounting the entire tale to his
audience. If not Homer, then certainly Demodocus. Demodo-

cus also sings like the Sirens for Odysseus, offering him knowledge of his words and deeds at Troy and knowledge of the order of the cosmos and the gods. Socrates knows the song well.
The Athenians have heard him sing it many times, and when
it does not put them to sleep, they find its incessant droning
quite irritating.

The *Phaedrus* concludes with a prayer, after which Socrates and
Phaedrus return to the city, going their separate ways (279b–c).
Plato bases Socrates' prayer on the trope of Odysseus's prayer
to Athena at the conclusion of book 6 of the *Odyssey* (324–27).
Both prayers occur in a sacred place outside the city, and both
are followed by the supplicant entering the city. Odysseus's
prayer asks that he might come among the Phaeacians as one
"loved and pitied." In other words, he hopes that, from love,
the Phaeacians might give him gifts worthy of him, and that,
from pity, they might grant him his homecoming. The prayer
is answered. The Phaeacians present him with many splendid
things and carefully stow them away for the voyage. However,
the ones that make him truly rich are not the sort that need
carting about: virtue and wisdom, or strength of character and
mind, the gifts of Arete and Alcinous. They are his, but he
does not fully possess them until he returns to Ithaca. When
he awakens on the shores of his homeland, he realizes that
he must hide his treasures. He prays to Athena for assistance,
and then again to the nymphs of the wellspring and cave in
which the things come to be stored (13.228–35, 356–60). Athena
also hides his gifts in another way: she transforms him into an
old beggar, dressing him in rags (13.429–38). In this guise—the
things within and the things without once again out of tune—
Odysseus enters the city. Plato's wording of the prayer Socrates
makes before returning to the city shows that he understands
there to be a relation between Odysseus's hopes before entering
the city of the Phaeacians, the prayer he makes to Athena for
assistance in hiding his gifts, and the significance of his return
to Ithaca in disguise. Indeed, the wording of Socrates' prayer

better corresponds to Homer's descriptions of the answers to Odysseus's prayers than it does to the prayers themselves.

Socrates prays to Pan and to the nymphs of the place, just as Odysseus prays to Athena and to the nymphs of the cave in which he hides his treasures. Socrates prays for harmony between internal and external things. But what sort of disharmony might lead to this prayer? His words do not express a longing for virtue similar to Odysseus's longing before entering the city of the Phaeacians. They are spoken more from an understanding of the need to renew virtue constantly. In the imagery of the *Odyssey,* the gifts he has received from the rulers of the heavenly city have already been hidden in his nymph cave; the setting for his omphallic travels and the place in which he has stored the treasures collected along the way is his own soul *(pace* Porphyry, *De Antro Nympharum).* In the imagery of the *Phaedrus,* Socrates' previous psychic and noetic ascents have led to his acquisition of the finest virtues; however, no mortal can remain at the roof of the cosmos indefinitely, and the descent that necessarily follows every ascent shows that even the best of the virtues is imperfect. Socrates' prayer thus recognizes the constant need to set out again and return to the All *(Pan).*

Nonetheless, Socrates has sufficient virtue to be considered rich. There is no better man. And yet, despite his virtue, he is not recognized in his own city. Few Athenians know who he is. Certainly not Phaedrus: even when Socrates uncovered himself, Phaedrus could not see that the images of the palinode are images of Socrates' soul (cf. *Symposium* 216d–217a, 221d–222a). The sense of disharmony between internal and external things that Plato has Socrates mention in his prayer before returning to Athens is thus intended to recall the circumstances of Odysseus's return to his city in the guise of an ugly beggar. Through Plato's artful reworking of Homer's imagery, the mist is lifted and the dialogue between Socrates and Phaedrus by the plane tree and stream that resembles the enchanting encounter between Odysseus and Nausicaa in a similarly pastoral setting is revealed to have more affinity to the scene of Odysseus sitting against the trunk of an olive tree near the nymph cave on the shores of Ithaca, plotting with Athena how best to deal with the shameless suitors who are ruining his household and his city.

When Socrates concludes his prayer, Phaedrus says he shares in it, but his heart is not in his words. The day has been one long disappointment for him. It began well enough, reading through Lysias's text again and again. As soon as he met Socrates, however, things gradually got worse: first the unsatisfying imitation of Lysias's text; then an unnecessary and rather long-winded recantation; then a difficult discussion of rhetoric that had nothing at all to do with eros; and now a prayer—thankfully, a short one. Plato shows that Phaedrus is less and less engaged in the conversation with Socrates by the manner in which he changes Phaedrus's role as the dialogue proceeds: Phaedrus is first cast as Nausicaa to Socrates' Odysseus, then one of Nausicaa's handmaidens (243e), then someone swimming backward in the wrong direction (264a), and then as an extra, no better than one of Odysseus's crew with melted wax in his ears. By the end of the dialogue, he seems to be entirely absent: if the prayer to Pan and the nymphs in which Phaedrus claims to share is understood as a reference to Athena and Odysseus planning a return to the city, then Socrates is alone with the god beside the tree.

When Socrates and Phaedrus part company, Phaedrus returns to Lysias, who is staying with Epicrates in a house that had previously been owned by Morychus. It might have been anticipated from previous encounters, but Phaedrus's inauspicious destination suggests that he has remained unaffected by anything Socrates has said. Even though the temple of Olympian Zeus is nearby, the house of Epicrates, the demagogue, previously the house of Morychus, the worst tragedian in Athens, must represent the lowest point yet reached in the steady decline of Athenian culture.[20] In sending Phaedrus on his way, Socrates tells him to take a message to Lysias. Phaedrus should tell him that the two of them "went down" (*katabante,*

20. See A. Philip, "Récurrences thématiques et topologie dans le «Phèdre» de Platon," *Revue de Métaphysique et de Morale* 86 (1981): 457.

278b) to the stream and the sacred place of the nymphs and recount the most important part of what was said there. A pleasant gibe. Phaedrus lacks the anamnetic skills of Socrates, who
recalled the whole of the *Republic*, beginning from the time he
"went down" to the Piraeus with Glaucon; he lacks the devo-
tion to Socrates of Aristodemus, Apollodorus, and Phaedo, all
of whom worked hard to memorize important conversations
of their beloved; and he is quite unlikely to spend time with
Lysias as he spent it with Socrates, even if he were to have a
text of their conversation in hand. Plato has Socrates send the
barbed message to show the reader that Phaedrus and Lysias,
despite all they have heard from Socrates, are not yet past the
point at which the *Republic* begins.

Socrates walks beside Phaedrus as they return to Athens, but
they go different ways. Socrates is returning home after having left the city and journeyed far. In this sense, the *Phaedrus* is
aesthetically complete and its ending is a resolution. However,
Socrates is also still searching for a homecoming, hoping that
he might soon come to a city in which he will be recognized.
In this sense, the *Phaedrus* is incomplete, and the imagery of its
conclusion leads to the beginning of the only other dialogue
set outside the city: the *Laws*. Socrates' walk toward Athens at
the end of the *Phaedrus* is Odysseus's walk toward the city of
the Phaeacians, and it is Odysseus's walk toward Ithaca, and
it is both together. Taken together, Ithaca and Scheria become
Magnesia, the city in speech of the *Laws*, the heavenly city in
which Socrates, disguised as the Athenian Stranger, would be
graciously received, recognized for who he is,[21] and given the
most splendid of gifts.

21. Compare *Phaedrus* 275b, which cites *Odyssey* 19.162–63, and *Laws*
624b, which cites *Odyssey* 19.178–79, as well as the scholia at *Odyssey*
19.178, 23.167.

Home
and Bed

When Penelope recognizes Odysseus, and he is finally home, Athena arrests the dawn's early light for them. In the timeless moment, Odysseus would go to bed with his loving wife. However, his openhearted admission that Teiresias prophesied further trials for them on the day he "went down" to Hades draws out their conversation a while; the wise Penelope, loving him for more than the dangers he had passed, asks to hear of them (*Odyssey* 23.241–62). Teiresias had truthfully foretold the obstacles and adversities he and his companions would have to overcome if they were ever to return home (11.100–120), but he also spoke of a further journey Odysseus must undertake (11.121–34) and of the strange manner of Odysseus's death (11.134–37). Odysseus recounts the latter parts of the prophecy for

Penelope, "concealing nothing" (*oud' epikeusō*, 23.265). He must travel until he discovers a people who do not know the sea. The sign of which Teiresias told him—Odysseus emphasizes it by his repeated remark that he will not conceal it *(oude se keusō)* from Penelope—is that the oar he carries on his "bright shoulder," the oar that acts for ships as "wings" *(ptera)* do for birds, will be mistaken for something else (23.267–75). Once he has found them, Odysseus must plant the oar in the ground and return home, honoring "all the gods in order" (23.281). Death will then come to him in his old age, "from the sea," in an "altogether unwarlike way" (23.281–84). As their bed is being prepared, Penelope says that she understands Teiresias's words to mean there is hope that Odysseus will escape from evils (23.285–87).

In the *Republic*, Plato has Socrates recollect the entirety of the previous night's events for his anonymous friend. "I went down yesterday to the Piraeus," he begins, and his friend listens patiently as Socrates recalls everything that was said, concealing nothing, to the end of the Pamphylian Er's "saving tale" (*Republic* 621b–c). Socrates speaks as Odysseus does with Penelope, recounting the difficult trials that delayed his homecoming. He speaks openly to someone who recognizes him as Penelope recognized her husband: perhaps to Plato himself, and similarly to any reader who loves him as Plato did. And the dramatic force of Socrates' first word, evoking Odysseus's revelation of Teiresias's prophecy, should prompt his true friend to ask him what other trials must be faced before there can be an escape from evils.

In Plato's use of Teiresias's prophecy as a symbol across several of the dialogues, showing their relation, the *Republic* might be taken as the story of Socrates' wanderings and homecoming, and the *Laws* the story of his subsequent travels. The tale of his death "from the sea" begins with the *Timaeus* and *Critias*, when Alcibiades sails into the Piraeus during the celebration of the Plynteria, and reaches its unexpectedly tranquil conclusion in the *Phaedo*, when the wait for Socrates' execution ends with the return of the Athenian ship sent on a sacred mission to Delos (*Phaedo* 58a–c). Several centuries before Plato composed the dialogues, the trope of Odysseus's later voyages and mysterious death had been taken as the basis for new epics by poets who thought the *Odyssey* to be an episodic and incomplete work: we know of the *Telegonia*, for example, in which Odysseus is killed by a son he is said to have had with Circe. Plato reads Homer differently, however, with a fine appreciation of the poet's richly textured symbols and subtle techniques of composition. For him, the *Odyssey* is not incomplete. If anything, Plato would likely agree with the interpretive tradition that maintains the *Odyssey* should end when the servants have finished the preparations and Odysseus and Penelope finally go to bed (*Odyssey* 23.296 and scholia). In the moment of their intimacy and embrace, the erotics of recognition underlying Odysseus's recounting of Teiresias's prophecy for Penelope is far more important than the literal sense of the words for understanding the meaning of what is revealed. A similar tension between what Socrates says and his relation to the one he addresses—a tension between the "said" and the "saying"—pervades the *Republic* and the *Phaedrus*, breaking now and then, most strikingly in the revelations of Socrates' palinode.

Teiresias is a sphinx. Penelope understands the significance of his words before Odysseus does, if not as soon as she hears them, then certainly at some time before dawn, as they take delight in one another's company again. She tells him of all she endured (23.300–305), and he recounts his travels, concealing neither the nature of his relations with Circe and Calypso nor the gifts he received from the Phaeacians who honored and loved him (23.306–43). There will not be another voyage. Penelope's love informs her understanding, and she is certain that Odysseus is home. The part of Teiresias's enigmatic prophecy that troubles Odysseus has already been fulfilled. It remains for him only to solve its riddle and recognize that he has already discovered the people who know nothing of the sea. The Phaeacians, whom Teiresias does not name explicitly in his description of the travails before Odysseus's homecoming, have magical ships whose oars are like wings. If Odysseus were to carry one of these oars on his "bright *(phaidimōi)* shoulder" (23.275), the best of the Phaeacians *(Phaiēkōn)* would surely see it as his wing. The moment Penelope recognizes him, Odysseus should also know he is home. When they first embrace, in tears, she sees him as he sees her: in Homer's radiant description, she sees him as the welcoming shore appears to a man desperately swimming to escape Poseidon's wrecking of his ship (23.231–40; cf. 5.391–99, 8.523–31). The erotics of recognition reveals to him that Ithaca is Scheria and Penelope is Nausicaa.

There will not be another voyage, if all goes well. Odysseus must realize the full significance of what has happened to him during his travels, and his disordered household and kingdom must be brought toward the order of the Phaeacian regime through prudent decisions. Teiresias said that the people he is to seek out will think that his oar is an *athērēloigos* (23.275): literally a "destroyer of corn," a winnowing fan, if the oar is seen as a common wooden tool, and just as literally a "destroyer of weapons" if the oar is seen as a wing. When the wings of eros sprout, the soul becomes altogether unwarlike. It does not take arms against a sea of troubles, but with wings as swift as thoughts of love, it takes flight to end them. Not by escaping them—worldly evils always remain—but by better understanding what might be done. Odysseus melted in tears when Demodocus exposed his murderous brutality during the sack of Troy. The same insight should guide his actions at home. And yet, the Cyclopean insolence and vulgarity of the suitors who have attempted to ruin his household and corrupt the regime are intolerable. Teiresias's prophecy gave him divine sanction to punish them with death if necessary, but that was to be an end to the violence (11.118–23). In a moment of anger and weakness, Odysseus forgets and oversteps the boundary: he allows Ithaca to begin a descent into the barbarism of civil war (23.348–70). He would walk through his own city, like the murderous Ares, o'er-sized with coagulate gore. Athena cries out, terrifying the assembled warriors into dropping their weapons, and commands them to settle matters "without blood" (24.528–35).

Deep in his rage, Odysseus does not hear her. Zeus must bring him to peace by blasting a lightning bolt at his feet (24.537–44).

The evidence of his lapse notwithstanding, Odysseus's shamanistic travels are complete within the tale told in the *Odyssey*. However, his final insight, the insight into the relation of the spiritual and political aspects of his travels, the relation of eros to political justice, is not stated explicitly. It is left for the reader to determine. In Plato's presentation of Socrates as the greater hero there are no comparable shameful lapses: Socrates has overcome Odysseus's last vice, the love of honor (*Republic* 620c). Furthermore, Socrates always already understands the things that Odysseus struggles to learn. The tale of Odysseus's wanderings and homecoming is refigured across the dialogues, but Socrates' travels are complete before any one of the dialogues begins. Socrates has always already attained the end. It is his interlocutor, and Plato's reader, the companion on the journey, whose homecoming remains in doubt.

In the *Phaedrus*, the scene of Odysseus's encounter with Nausicaa is refigured for Socrates' discussion with Phaedrus, but the palinode shows that Socrates already understands the Phaeacians to be the people who mistake oars for wings and honor all the gods "in order." As the scene is played out, Phaedrus fails in his role and the reader must take it over. In the *Timaeus* and *Critias*, the scene of Odysseus's reception at the Phaeacian court is refigured for Socrates' entertaining day at Critias's house. As the scene is played out with Critias and Timaeus all too eager to instruct Socrates, Plato's art shows the reader that hidden in Socrates' laconic remarks and long silences there is already an understanding of everything Demodocus's songs reveal to Odysseus. And in the *Republic*, the dialogue in which the spiritual and political aspects of Odysseus's travels are refigured for a parallel discussion of types of souls and types of cities, Glaucon, one of Socrates' most courageous companions, loses his homecoming at the last moment when he slaughters the cattle of Helios: he refuses to follow Socrates to a vision of the good beyond being, and thus precludes a resolution of the night's discussions in a matching

description of a just city. As the scene is played out, it remains
for the reader to recognize that Glaucon's dismissal of Socrates'
vision traps him in the *kallipolis*, and that the unresolved discussions of the *Republic* are taken up elsewhere. Plato's refiguring
of Odysseus's recognition by Penelope as the relation between
Socrates and the friend to whom he recounts the night's discussions is the reader's sign. There is another journey to undertake. But more than that: the erotics of recognition in the scene
also reveals that there need not be another journey. Odysseus
had already returned from the heavenly city of the Phaeacians
before telling Penelope of his travels and Teiresias's prophecy.
Similarly, Socrates has already returned from the city in speech
of the *Laws* before the discussions of the *Republic* begin. Magnesia takes the account of the heavens in the *Phaedrus* as the
paradigm for its political order. Magnesia, and not the *kallipolis*,
is the heavenly city that Plato has Socrates say he has founded
within his soul (*Republic* 592a–b).

Odysseus is not home until Penelope accepts him, and she will
not accept him until he passes the most revealing of tests. When
they first speak privately, she asks the much-traveled stranger
who he is; and on learning from his avoidance of the question
that he had met Odysseus in Crete, she asks him what clothes
Odysseus had worn. Penelope had given him the clothes herself, so the stranger's accurate description lends credence to his
report of Odysseus's imminent homecoming (*Odyssey* 19.105–
307). As he is being washed by the old nurse Eurykleia, who
recognizes his scar but must keep her silence, Penelope decides
to trust his word. She says she intends to announce a contest to
the suitors: she will marry whoever can string Odysseus's bow
and shoot an arrow—as he often did, from far off—through the
handles of twelve axes stood in a row, resembling the timbers
that hold the keel of a ship being built (19.570–80). The next
day, the suitors fail even to string the bow. The stranger asks to
test his strength, and while the suitors dispute his right to do
so, Penelope retires. She does not see him easily string it and

shoot the arrow through the axes; she does not see the suitors turn pale in fear; and she does not see Odysseus, with the help of his son and those of the household who have remained loyal to him, kill them all, sparing only the herald and the singer (22.330–80). When Penelope is woken by the nurse, who tells her that Odysseus is in the house and has killed the suitors, she does not accept the news until Eurykleia adds that the stranger had been Odysseus in disguise (23.1–38). And yet, she hesitates as she goes down to meet him. The house has been cleaned hastily, but Odysseus's clothing is fouled by the blood and filth of the slaughter. Penelope remains silent, even though the man does look like her husband (23.85–95). She does not yet recognize him. The proofs are still inadequate. Not his description of the clothing she had given him, not the physical resemblance, not his use of the contest to kill the hateful suitors—any strong and clever man can be a successful murderer—not even if he were to say explicitly that he is Odysseus and her husband.

When Odysseus returns from bathing, freshly clothed, and Penelope remains silent, he loses patience and asks that a bed be made up for him. Penelope then speaks. She asks Eurykleia to bring down Odysseus's own bed, the one he had built himself years ago (23.163–80). When Odysseus erupts in anger, demanding to know how the bed he constructed to be unmovable can now be moved about, Penelope bursts into tears and kisses him in recognition (23.181–208). And when Penelope explains to him that her need to be cautious and deceptive was as great as his, Odysseus also weeps, recognizing his wife's virtue and knowing that he is finally home (23.209–40). However, Odysseus's description of their bed is a true proof, and Penelope's explanation of the test is a sincere one, only if they have both kept faith and revealed nothing of the bed and its construction to anyone during the past twenty years. The most intimate things cannot be tested, and for Odysseus and Penelope they are never in doubt.

Homer describes Odysseus's homecoming to recall Odysseus's reception among the Phaeacians. Penelope is both Nausicaa and Arete; Odysseus defeats the suitors, both in a contest, as he had silenced Laodamas and Euryalos by throwing a discus, and in a cunning ambush, as a similar device, described in Demodocus's songs, had brought about the slaughter of the Trojans; and then, the bed. Homer's description of the bed that Odysseus and Penelope share makes it comparable to Hephaestus's bed. Odysseus built his marriage bed by using a living olive tree for one of its bedposts, trimming it down with an ax and joining it to the rest of the bed frame with an auger. Only a god could move it, Odysseus says. If some man attempted it, he would have to kill the still-living tree by cutting it off at the trunk (23.183–204).[1] An omphallic tree as a bedpost; the subordination of skill and technique in its construction to the preservation of the tree; the erotics of maintaining a marriage bed that is unmovable, unless a god were to do it; equivalent machinations of betrayal in the destruction of the bed and adultery. Odysseus's bed and Hephaestus's bed are quite similar. However, Hephaestus's bed was not as well maintained. Ares defiled Hephaestus's bed by seducing Aphrodite, but Ares' rude art alone could not have brought him success. Aphrodite defiled the bed by accepting the advances of her dull seducer, but there must have been reason for her dissatisfaction. One reason is evident in the pride Hephaestus takes in his clever construction of a net to entrap the lovers, a pride much greater than any shame he felt in being seen by the gods as a cuckold. Hephaestus violates his own "dear bed" with his even dearer devices (8.277). When Demodocus sings of Ares and Aphrodite, Odysseus is reminded of his marriage bed. His songs of Troy are thus all the more effective in teaching him how his guile had led him to become like the murderous

1. Scholars concerned to interpret the bed's construction usually claim that it is a symbol of the relation between the natural and conventional aspects of marriage, as commonly understood. For Wendy Doniger, the bed is a "metaphor for marriage, which cages and codifies the living force of sexual passion but keeps it alive" ("The Homecomings of Odysseus and Nala," in *Literary Imagination, Ancient and Modern: Essays in Honor of David Grene*, ed. T. Breyfogle [Chicago: University of Chicago Press, 1999], 93). For Eva Brann, a bed without a "vigorous" tree for a bedpost would be a symbol of a "rootless, placeless, loveless marriage without natural foundations" (*Homeric Moments: Clues to Delight in Reading the "Odyssey" and the "Iliad"* [Philadelphia: Paul Dry Books, 2002], 288).

Ares. And when Penelope tests Odysseus by reminding him of their marriage bed, she does the same. But with one remarkable difference: Penelope reminds Odysseus of what he knew before he set sail for Troy.

Plato refigures Homer's beds in several dialogues, moving them about with flawless technique. In the beginning of the *Timaeus*, Socrates is not recognized for who he is, even when he draws attention to his fresh, festive clothes. It does not come as a surprise, therefore, when the erotics implicit in Demodocus's song of Ares and Aphrodite is concealed in Plato's refiguring of Hephaestus's worldview for Timaeus's cosmology. Timaeus is all net, and no bed. And worse: using the symbolism of Odysseus's bed, Plato suggests that Timaeus's technique destroys the living tree that is the bed's foundation. Odysseus constructs his bed with an ax and an auger, preserving the life of the omphallic tree; it takes only one swing of an ax to kill it. Timaeus's skill is division, the ax and nothing else. His cosmos, therefore, is nothing but parts; it is not unified and moved by eros; it does not live. In the *Phaedrus*, in contrast, the omphallic tree—the *platanos*—is a constant presence. The bed might not be mentioned explicitly, but the erotic tension of Odysseus's encounter with Nausicaa pervades Plato's rewriting and breaks through in the palinode's description of eros flowing through all things in the cosmos and overflowing in the souls of lovers. In less breathless style, Plato restates the techniques that Odysseus uses in constructing his bed in Socrates' account of dialectic: division and collection, Odysseus's ax and auger; the proper use of the tools, his shaping of a "heaven-high" tree; the end for which the technical means are used, the erotics of the marriage; and, finally, recognition of the ultimate superiority of the god. In the *Symposium*, the erotic aspects of Homer's beds are most evident in Aristophanes' comical genealogy of the human race (189c–193d). In a previous epoch, when double humans gave birth in the soil, like cicadas, and not in one another, Zeus attempted to solve the problem of their rebelliousness by applying his expertise in division and collection. He cut them in half, souls as well as bodies, and created eros. Eros is the longing in the soul to heal the wound

and become whole again by finding one's other half and cling-
ing to it forever. Zeus's original job is a bit botched, but once
human bodies are tweaked, things are as we now know them.
Plato's Aristophanes effortlessly generalizes the erotics of Demodocus's song to the human race. And he is all eros, no net.
He even has Hephaestus make a cameo appearance in the eulogy, but only to offer lovers his entirely redundant services
(192d–e).

Aristophanes and Agathon nod off at the end of the *Symposium*, too drunk and weary to follow Socrates' argument that
a knowledgeable and skilled poet should be able to write both
tragedy and comedy. Having no one to talk to, Socrates tucks
them in and spends the next day minding his own business before going home and to bed (223c–d). If the trail of the argument
lost in wine and forgetfulness were to be taken up, it would
lead to the comprehensive poetics of Plato's dialogues, which
subsume the forms of tragedy and comedy in the epic tale of
Socrates' philosophic life. Socrates is a hero of a different type,
a hero whose momentous words and deeds are disguised by
his prosaic way of speaking and his plain, everyday manner.

There is little of what is traditionally thought to be tragic or
comic in a life of inquiry, but such drama and humor as it does
possess are evident in an entertaining discussion that Socrates
has with Glaucon in the concluding book of the *Republic*. When
Socrates admits to being a "lover of poetry" who is "charmed"
to contemplate things "through Homer" (*di' Homērou theōrēis*),
he suggests that Glaucon might consider doing so as well
(607c–d). Glaucon has made many bold pronouncements during the night's conversation, not the least of which were his
criticisms and censorship of the poets, especially Homer. To
test his understanding of the nature of poetic imitation, Plato
has Socrates make him ponder different kinds of couches and
their relation to a couch made by a god. Socrates tests Glaucon's familiarity with Homer's beds, in other words. It is not
likely that Glaucon will recognize what is being asked of him.

Plato's presentation of the test is based on the scene of Penelope's testing of Odysseus, but he refigures the episode in the *Odyssey* as a comedy, reserving its dramatic intimacy for the trope of Socrates' relation to his silent, and amused, auditor. And if there is any doubt that one should expect Glaucon to become entangled in the paradoxes of Socrates' description of the couches, it is surely dispelled when Plato has Socrates preface the discussion with a caustic remark that Glaucon's understanding of imitation might be aided by his relatively "duller vision" (595c–596a).

Following Socrates' prompting, Glaucon readily agrees that there are three sorts of couches. The couch in a painting imitates a couch made by a craftsman, and the craftsman's couch imitates a couch made by the god. The couch made by the god is an original, the craftsman's couch is an imitation, and the painter's couch is thus an imitation of an imitation (596e–597e). Now, this cannot be altogether serious. Indeed, several objections to the argument, plainly evident to common sense, are suggested in Socrates' own elaborations (597b–c, 601c–d). What moves a god to make a couch at all? A need to use one? By what caprice or necessity does the god make only one couch? And when he sets out to make it, must he not imitate a preexisting idea of a couch? Are there three different sorts of couches or three ideas of a single couch or three understandings of a single idea of a couch? The puzzling features of the discussion are all consequences of its problematic first premise. The original is itself an imitation: the god's couch, as Socrates describes it, obviously imitates both the craftsman's couch and the painter's couch.[2] But why does Socrates use such an unclear image? Confusion about originals—mistaken remarks and identities—is a mainstay of comedy. And Socrates' deadpan delivery of the perplexing argument is intended to lead Glaucon into a muddle for

2. In the *Histories*, Herodotus says that the uppermost level of the ziggurat dedicated to Bel, the Babylonian Zeus, holds no representation or image of the god; however, it does hold "a couch of unusual size" for his convenience (1.181). Plato might well have used this account, or similar travelers' reports, as one of the sources for the imagery of Socrates' discussion.

humorous effect. However, there is another, more important reason for Socrates' teasing. Confusion about originals and the nature of imitation is also the basis of sophistry's power (596c–e). Although Glaucon has nothing but contempt for sophistry, his mistaking of the nature of philosophy leaves him open to its influence. Perhaps Socrates intends to do him some good with a few minutes of the right sort of puzzlement.

Penelope's doubts about the stranger who those around her claim is her husband are resolved when, in a passionate response to her deliberately misleading words, he proves to her that he knows the difference between the original, an imitation, and an imitation of an imitation. The simple distinction between the unique marriage bed Odysseus built—an original—and ordinary, movable beds—rather poor imitations—suffices to make Penelope's bed trick effective. But there is much more at stake. The marriage bed is also an imitation. Odysseus worked as a craftsman when he built it. By using the proper tools and techniques to preserve the life of the omphallic tree that is its foundation, Odysseus built his marriage bed to imitate the true original: not the bed of a god, imagined as a heavenly projection of an ordinary bed; not even the bed built by Hephaestus, for whom technique surpasses eros; but, rather, the unmovable itself. Odysseus's bed is a true imitation of a true original, and hence an original itself, standing apart from common beds by several removes.

Glaucon fails the bed test. A bit too rashly clever, perhaps, and willing to throw himself headlong into intellectual quandaries that ensnare him; and too much troubled by his imperfect eros as well (402d–403b, 474c–475b). It is no wonder, then, that he finds Socrates' account of the three couches baffling and that he ends up playing the part of one of the less sympathetic comic characters: the rejected suitor. But there is much more at stake in Socrates' bed test than some playful teasing intended to expose the man who would censor Homer as someone with an inadequate understanding of the nature of poetic imitation. Glaucon's failure also calls the entire night's discussion of the nature of justice into question.

When Socrates first saw a chance to escape the party at Cephalus's house, Glaucon and Adeimantus prevented him from
going home from the Piraeus, compelling him to stay until he
gave a proper explanation of why justice is preferable to injustice (357a–b). They insisted that Socrates explain the nature
of justice in itself, without regard to consequence (358b–367e),
disregarding Socrates' initial definition of justice as the sort of
good that is desirable both for its own sake and for what comes
from it (357b–358a). To appease them, Socrates took their understanding of justice as an original for an image: the order of
a just city. Then, to determine if the city they founded in speech
was indeed just, Socrates proposed that it be tested by taking
its form as the model for the order of a just soul (434d–435a).
But how is this an adequate test? The correspondence of the
image of an image to the image that is its original proves nothing. And how can the image of the just soul itself be tested? It
must be compared to the true original if any of this is to make
sense. Glaucon constrains Socrates to go about things his way,
but Socrates knows where the argument is leading: Glaucon's
"methods" will never get anywhere, he says when impatience
gets the better of him; there is another, "longer way" that must
be taken (435c–d). Glaucon's methods have produced an account of the just soul that is a true image of a true image of an
imperfect original: his initial understanding of justice and its
relation to the good. Socrates repeatedly attempts to lead him
away from it, but to no avail. When Socrates finally succeeds in
giving an account of the "longer way" (504b), the ascent toward
a vision of the good "beyond being" that produces true justice
in the soul, justice with consequence, Glaucon flatly dismisses
it as "daimonic hyperbole" (509b–c). Glauon's failure to follow
Socrates' persuasion and clarify his understanding of originals
and images is pitiable, but it is also "laughable," as Socrates
himself describes it to his friend (509c). When Socrates gives
Glaucon the opportunity to fail a second time, however, the result is entirely comic.

It is often embarrassing to miss the point of a joke. In the
awkward moment afterward, the temptation is strong to cover

one's chagrin by soberly denying that anything at all had been funny. In the history of Plato scholarship, alas, Socrates' banter with Glaucon about the god's couch is a joke that has gone sour. A pattern of original, imitation, and imitation of imitation has been abstracted from these passages in the *Republic* and used as the basis for much erudite speculation about Plato's "theory of forms" without giving consideration to the significance of Socrates' deliberately flawed original. Similarities have been recognized between this pattern of original and imitations and the cosmology of the *Timaeus*. Rightfully so: Plato does intend the reader to recall Socrates' image of the god building his couch when considering the point of Timaeus's story of the demiurge's construction of the cosmos in imitation of a divine paradigm. Similarities have also been recognized between the cosmology of the *Timaeus* and the construction of the *kallipolis* in the *Republic*. Again, rightfully so: the pattern of original and imitations stated in Socrates' account of the three couches underlies them both. The textual parallels, in themselves, are not reason enough to assume that Plato intended the dialogues to be interpreted through the limited understandings of Glaucon, Timaeus, and Critias. Plato's Socrates is not a metaphysical and political idealist, nor is Plato. Nevertheless, a tottering edifice of "Platonism" has been built up over the centuries from these and comparable passages in the dialogues, read with much gravity and ceremony by scholars unconcerned with cultivating a reputation for a sense of humor. It is well past time to pull the rug out from underneath the thing and let it cave in.

When Penelope tests Odysseus in private, she uses misleading words in her description of their marriage bed to allow the true intimacy of their relation to be revealed. Plato refigures the trope of the bed test twice in the *Republic:* the misleading words of Socrates' description of the three couches test Glaucon's sense of humor, but the intimacy of Socrates' narrative voice throughout the dialogue assumes that the joke, retold the next day, will be appreciated by the friend who already recognizes him for who he is. Unless we allow the *Republic* to address us as Socrates addresses his friend, understanding the erotics of recognition implicit in his first word, the dialogue will always seem remote and unfamiliar. The spirited humor and dramatic weight of Socrates' words will be misconstrued, and the epic significance of Plato's account of his life will remain buried in a rubble of doctrinal misinterpretations.

Odysseus is twice tested by Penelope. The bed test, given in private, is preceded by Penelope's public contest requiring all competitors to attempt to string Odysseus's bow and shoot an arrow through the handles of twelve axes stood in a row. If there is a man present who can do the things Odysseus could do, he will be revealed before all of Ithaca as Odysseus, and Penelope will publicly accept him as her husband. In Penelope's understanding, it is sufficient for a man to meet the challenges of the test; in Odysseus's understanding, it is also an occasion to throw off his disguise and slaughter the suitors. As it happens, Penelope goes to bed and does not see Odysseus both pass and fail the test; when she awakens, therefore, she cannot be certain if the man standing before her, his clothes fouled with blood, is truly her husband. Another, more intimate test is necessary.

Plato also tests the reader twice in the *Republic*. The first word of the dialogue—*katebēn*, "I went down"—is the more private and intimate test. The public test, a second chance to recognize who Socrates is, comes at the very end of the dialogue. Plato refigures Penelope's archery contest in Socrates' recounting of Er's tale. When Odysseus strung his bow and shot an arrow through the axes, the suitors knew immediately who he was, despite his disguise. Odysseus appeared before them in the instant, returned from his travels. Although they did not live to hear the tale, Odysseus had returned to Ithaca from journeys to Hades, the realm of the dead, and Scheria, the land of the Phaeacians. In Homer's use of shamanistic imagery, Odysseus's arrow, shot from afar, strikes its target like Zeus's lightning bolt; the ax handles, aligned perfectly, like the timbers that hold the keel of a ship being built, are the points at which the axis mundi intersects the heavenly spheres, as Zeus might see them from the hyperouranian region; and in the moment of the arrow's impact, the return and rebirth of Odysseus are indistinguishable.

In Plato's refiguring of Homer's imagery, the gods allow Er the Pamphylian, the man of all tribes, to return alive from the daimonic region in which the souls of the dead are judged and choose new lives before being reborn in order that its mysteries might become known to all people. When it is time for them to choose, the souls of the dead travel to an omphalos that recalls the place on the roof of the cosmos at which the axis mundi bursts through into the heavens. They see the axis as a column of light, binding all things together, "like the undergirders of triremes" (616b–c). After they have all chosen the lives they think best, the earth quakes, thunder sounds, and in a flash they travel like lightning bolts or shooting stars along the axis mundi to their rebirth (621a–b). In Socrates' telling of Er's tale, the gods allow him to see only one such event. On that day, Odysseus's soul is the last to choose a new life. Having over-come its last vice, the love of honor, it rejoices to find the life of a man who "minds his own business" (620c). In the flash of a lightning bolt, it shoots along the axis mundi, through the spheres of the cosmos, and is reborn. And in the moment of the arrow's impact, Socrates stands before us, revealed as the new Odysseus. When Odysseus hit his target, the suitors had good reason to pale in fear. Socrates returns from his further journeys unarmed, always content to go home and to bed.

Index

Achilles, 51, 52, 53
Adam, James, 18*n14*
Adeimantus, 27, 28, 35, 123
Agamemnon, 51
Agathon: in *Symposium*, 54, 71–72, 120
Alcibiades, 29–30, 29*n6*, 31, 31*n7*, 32, 32*n9*, 35, 36, 42–43, 63; and Critias, 29, 29*n6*, 36, 37–38, 38*n11*, 63; Xenophon on, 38*n11*
Alcinous, 34, 35, 37, 38, 52, 62, 77, 102, 107
Anaxagoras, 73
Aphrodite: and Ares, in Demodocus's second song, 41, 43–44, 55, 91, 118; refigured in *Timaeus*, 45–46
Apollodorus, 110
Ares: and Aphrodite, in Demodocus's second song, 41, 43–44, 55, 91, 118; refigured in *Timaeus*, 45–46; Odysseus likened to, 52, 53, 62, 114, 118–19

Arete, 34, 37, 38, 77, 102, 107; and Penelope, 117
Aristodemus, 110
Aristophanes: *Frogs*, 32*n9*; in *Symposium*, 119–20
Aristotle: *Politics* 1267b21–22, 61
Artemis, 97, 98–99; and Nausicaa, 80, 85, 87, 96
Athena, 97, 98, 102, 114; in Atlantis story, 59, 61; and Nausicaa, 77, 78, 80, 85; and Odysseus, 78, 102, 103, 107, 108–9, 111, 114–15
—Festivals: Panathena, 28; Plynteria, 28, 28*n3*, 30, 31, 31*n8*, 33, 36, 53, 63, 112
Atlantis, 56, 57–62; and *kallipolis*, 56, 59; textual lineage of story, 56–57, 58; political concerns of Critias's story, 59, 60–62; antithesis of Athens, 60–61; and *Phaedrus*, 73, 94
Auditors or readers: of *Republic*, 1, 6, 25, 36, 41, 53, 112, 116, 121,

127